Easy-to-Make

FAIRY TALE DOLLS

& All the Trimmings

Jodie Davis

♥

Photography by Glenn Moody

Williamson Publishing • Charlotte, Vermont 05445

Library of Congress
Cataloging-in-Publication Data

Davis, Jodie, 1959-
    Easy-to-make fairy tale dolls & all the
    trimmings / Jodie Davis; photography by
    Glenn Moody.
        p.   cm. Includes bibliographical references.
ISBN 0-913589-70-5 : $13.95
        1. Dollmaking.   2. Cloth dolls. 3. Dolls clothes
    — Patterns.   I. Title.   II. Title: Fairy tale
dolls & all the trimmings.
        TT175.D383   1993
        745.592'21—dc20   92-43454 CIP

Cover illustration: Loretta Trezzo Braren
Cover design: Trezzo-Braren Studio
Photography: Glenn Moody
Project diagrams: Jodie Davis
Printing: Capital City Press

Jodie Davis is author of the following
Williamson titles:
Easy-To-Make Teddy Bears & All The Trimmings
Easy-to-Make Cloth Dolls & All The Trimmings
Easy-To-Make Stuffed Animals & All The Trimmings
Easy-To-Make Endangered Species To Stitch & Stuff

Williamson Publishing Co.
Charlotte, Vermont 05445
(800) 234-7891

Manufactured in the United States of America

10 9 8 7 6 5 4 3

Notice: The information contained in this book
is true, complete and accurate to the best of our
knowledge. All recommendations and suggestions
are made without any guarantees on the part of
the author or Williamson Publishing. The author
and publisher disclaim all liability incurred in
connection with the use of this information.

C O N T E N T S

DEDICATION

To my parents,
for a fairy tale childhood.
To Lee,
for the sequel.

We all share a common heritage in the form of fairy tales and nursery rhymes passed down through many generations. They delight us as youngsters, and as adults we rediscover these friends while reading the stories to our own children and grandchildren, appreciating them all the more.

Follow these step-by-step instructions to create a fairyland full of dream-like characters. Enlist them as story-telling aids and the tales will spring to life. Cloth doll fanciers, children, and adults alike will treasure these creations as cherished collectibles.

Jodie Davis

♥

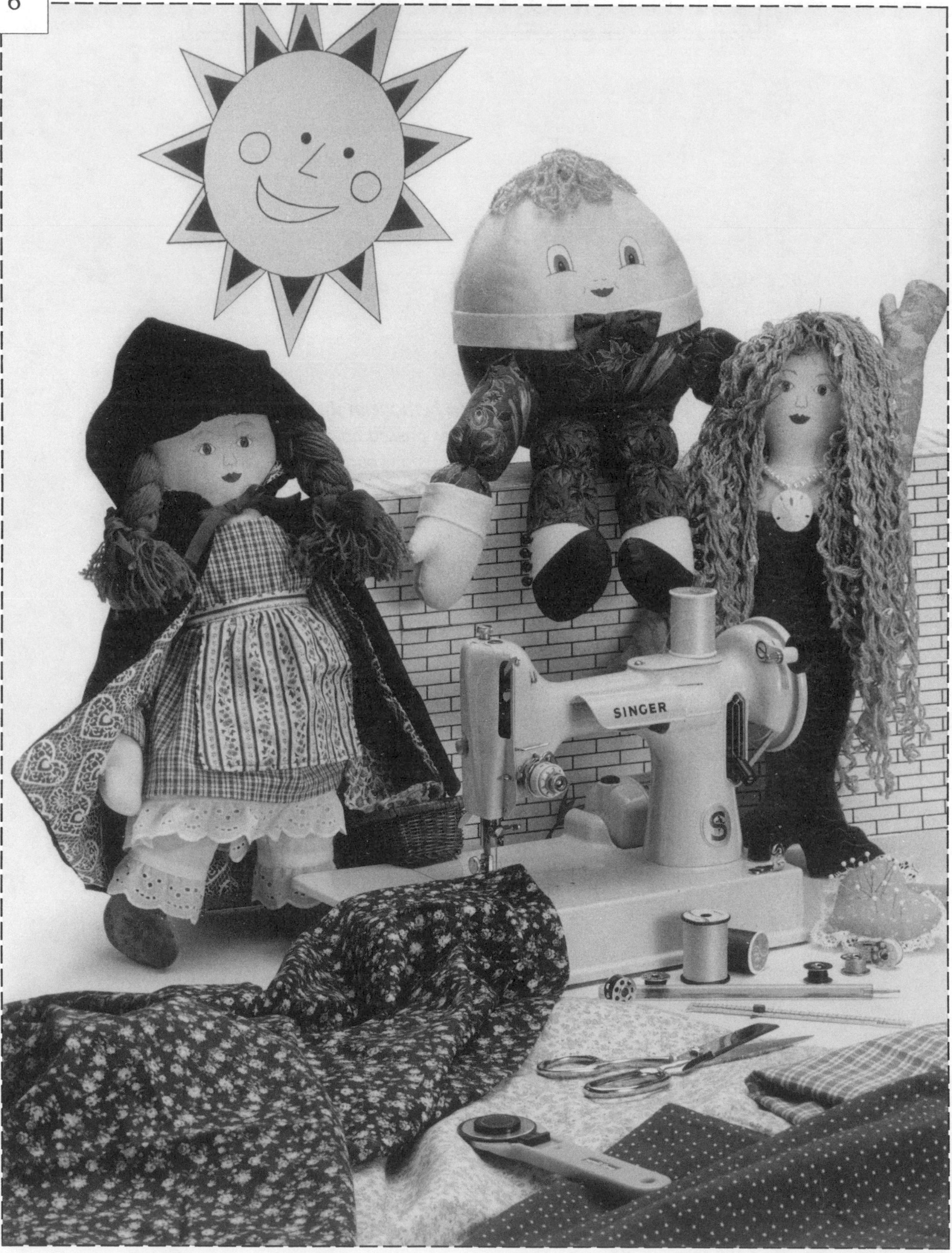
SINGER

♥

The Basics

This chapter provides the fundamentals for constructing the characters in this book. Several general sewing reference books are listed in the bibliography at the back of the book. You will find them in your local library or bookstore. These will give you a more thorough review of sewing basics.

Before you begin your project, assemble all the necessary tools and materials, and then follow the instructions one step at a time.

♥

GENERAL SUPPLIES

Essential

Sewing machine: Depending upon the brand of machine you use, choose a size 80 or 12 needle. Use a normal stitch length for most sewing. Shorten the stitches for smaller, curved areas, such as hands and toes. This will make sewing easier and smoother.

Bent-handle dressmaker's shears: Good, quality shears, 7" or 8" in length, are recommended for general sewing purposes. Reserve these shears for cutting fabric only, as paper will dull them quickly.

Scissors: Used for cutting paper, cardboard, and other materials, these inexpensive scissors will save your shears from a lot of wear and tear.

Permanent marking pen: For drawing and outlining dolls' faces when painting, nothing beats a Pigma Micron™. I use a size 01 in black or brown (see Sources).

Dressmaker's tracing paper: Used for transferring markings from patterns to fabric.

Dressmaker's tracing wheel: A device used with the tracing paper.

Straight pins or paper weights: To hold paper pattern pieces in place as you cut the fabric out.

General purpose thread: The all-purpose size 50 will fill most of your general hand and machine sewing needs. Some people insist on cotton thread but I find that polyester or cotton-wrapped polyester are stronger and slide through the fabric more easily.

Waxed dental floss or quilting thread: Perfect for closing the seams of The Three Bears.

Glue: A general purpose white glue made for fabric, felt, wood, and paper is available at any dime, crafts, or fabric store under a variety of brand names.

Paper: For clothing and other patterns.

Nice to Have

Seam ripper: A sharp, pointed tool used to tear out temporary basting stitches and seams. I list this as non-essential because you can substitute the thread clipper listed below.

Pinking shears: These cut a ravel-resistant zigzag. They are used for finishing seams. A good choice is the 7$^{1}/_{2}$" size.

Thread clippers: A variation on a small pair of scissors, thread clippers are made by a number of companies and are handy for trimming threads at the sewing machine, for clipping into seam allowances, and for making buttonholes. If you do much sewing, I highly recommend having a pair on hand.

Thimble: This is listed as non-essential though many, including myself, will argue that this little piece of equipment is, in fact, essential in guiding the needle and guarding against painful pinpricks.

SEWING TECHNIQUES

Darts

Fold the fabric along the center line of the dart, right sides together. Beginning at the raw edges, or widest point of the dart, sew the dart along the broken lines to the point and backstitch to secure the stitching. For clothing, press the dart to one side.

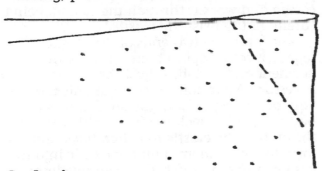

Gathering

Using a long stitch, make a row of stitches between the marks indicated on the pattern, leaving the thread tails long enough to grasp so you can pull them. Repeat another row close to the first stitching.

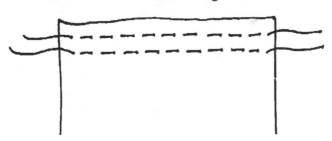

Pin the two pieces together, matching the dots on the two pattern pieces as indicated. Pull up the threads to gather the fabric and loop the thread tails around the pins at each end. Adjust the gathers evenly and smoothly. Baste the seam and stitch.

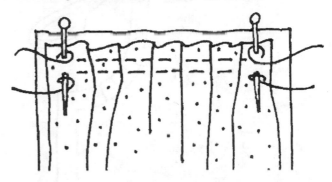

Cutting Out the Dolls and Clothing

As noted at the beginning of the instructions for the dolls and clothing, ¼" seam allowances are included in the patterns for the clothing, but not for the doll body patterns.

Instead of including the seam allowances in the body patterns, the pattern lines are the stitching lines. Trace around the pattern pieces onto the muslin body fabric. Then, stitch just inside the traced lines. Now cut the body part out, using a ⅛" seam allowance. This is a very accurate method and results in a small seam allowance that creates a smooth, professional finished product.

Trimming and Clipping Seams

After stitching a seam, seam allowances are trimmed and clipped for a number of reasons. For clothing, trimming with pinking shears will reduce the bulk of the seam and, in some fabrics, prevent raveling of the raw edges. Clipping into the seam allowances of convex, or outward, curves permits the edges to spread when the item is turned right side out. Notching the seam allowances on concave, or inward, curves allows the edges to draw in when the item is turned right side out. Trimming across corners insures a smooth finished seam and square, crisp corners.

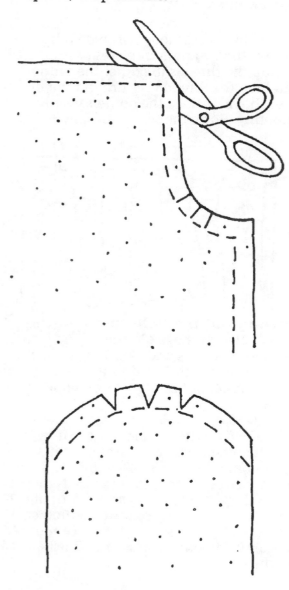

Elastic Casings

The casing is a tunnel of turned under fabric enclosing flat elastic which is stretched to fit snugly around the body.

To make an elastic casing, the edge of the garment is pressed under ¼". Then the edge is turned and pressed under an additional ¾" to the desired amount. The lower edge of the casing is then machine-stitched in place, leaving a ½"-wide opening for threading the elastic. Machine-stitch a second row of stitching close to the top fold.

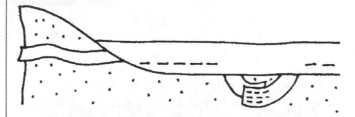

Cut a length of elastic as indicated in the instructions for the garment. Attach a safety pin to one end of the elastic, push it into the casing and work it through the casing, being careful not to twist the elastic.

Safety pin the two ends of the elastic together, overlapping them ½ ". Try the garment on the doll. Adjust the elastic if necessary. Your doll's measurements may vary according to how you stuff it, so it is best to double check the fit. Machine-stitch the ends of the elastic together, back and forth to secure them. Pull the elastic into the casing. Machine-stitch the opening closed, being careful not to catch the elastic in the stitching.

STITCH DICTIONARY

Basting Stitch

This long, ¼" by hand or longest possible by machine, temporary stitch is used for marking and for stitching together two pieces of fabric to make sure they fit properly before the final stitching.

Running Stitch

This stitch is similar to the basting stitch, though it is a shorter, even stitch, for fine, permanent seaming.

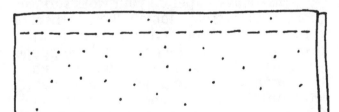

Topstitch

Longer than a regular sewing stitch, the topstitch is applied from the right side of the finished item, and is for decorative or functional purposes (to secure casings, zippers, and facings), and often both.

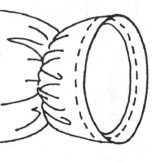

Overhand or Whipstitch

This is used to join two finished edges, as when closing the turned under edges of the ear.

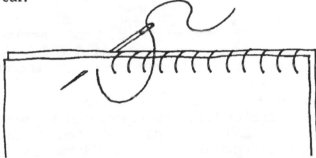

Ladder Stitch

Use this stitch to close the openings in the dolls' and animals' bodies. This easy stitch results in professional-looking seam closures.

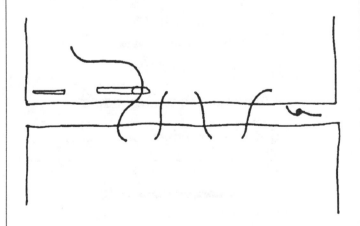

Staystitching

Staystitching is simply a row of small machine stitches along the stitching line.

Backstitch

Formed by inserting the needle behind the point where the thread emerges from the previous stitch. This is used for outlining features, like eyebrows.

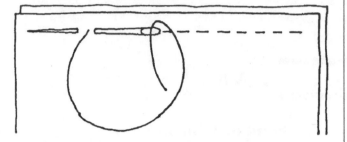

Satin Stitch

These decorative stitches, usually of colored thread or embroidery floss, are essentially stitches worked side-by-side, following an outline.

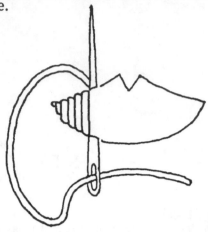

MAKING PATTERNS

All of the patterns in this book are shown in their actual size. It is suggested that you make your doll patterns out of a heavy cardboard, such as oak tag or cereal boxes, as accuracy is extremely important. By tracing around the cardboard pieces you will transfer the patterns very accurately. Paper will suffice for the clothing patterns as you will pin them to the fabric and cut out the pieces.

MATERIALS

Tracing paper

Dressmaker's tracing paper

Cardboard or paper for patterns

TIP: Manilla envelopes and resealable sandwich bags are great places to store your patterns. Label them and store them away for future use.

INSTRUCTIONS

1. Lay a piece of tracing paper over the pattern in the book. Carefully trace the pattern onto the tracing paper, including all pattern markings.

2. Lay the cardboard or, for clothing patterns, heavy paper on your work surface (not the dining room table!). Place a sheet of carbon paper on top and your tracing paper over that. To avoid the possiblity of slippage you may wish to tape the two top sheets to the bottom cardboard or paper, or to the work surface. With a pencil or dressmaker's wheel trace the pattern, pressing firmly. Pick up a corner of the two top layers to be sure that the pattern is being transferred clearly to the bottom surface. Transfer all markings to the pattern.

3. Cut out your pattern. Mark the name of the pattern piece and the name of the doll or garment on it.

DYEING THE BODY FABRIC

Give your doll's body a slight skin tone with this quick and easy dyeing technique.

Rinse the muslin with hot water. Set aside. Fill the sink with enough hot water (let it run from the tap for a minute before closing the drain stopper so it will be the hottest) to cover the fabric. Add a tablespoon each of peach and rose pink powdered or liquid dye. Mix well. For brown or other colored skin tone, use brown or another color dye similar to desired result.

Cut a swatch of muslin. Swish in the dye bath for a minute. Put in the dryer. Check the color. Too light? Add more dye. Too dark? Add more hot water.

When you are satisfied with the color, immerse the fabric and stir for a few minutes to dye the fabric evenly. Remove from the dye bath. Rinse. Put in the clothes dryer. When the fabric is almost dry, remove from the dryer and press.

SEWING THE DOLLS

A short machine stitch is recommended for sewing the dolls. Since a lot of strain will be placed on the seams, especially around the tight curves of the hands and feet, these smaller stitches will add the strength needed to withstand stuffing and loving.

STUFFING

Begin with a quality stuffing — one of even, fluffy consistency. Always begin at the extremities — hands or toes — using smaller bits of stuffing for small parts, packing them in tightly. Gradually use larger chunks of stuffing as you progress to the larger parts of the doll. Handfuls of stuffing produce less lumping. Pack the stuffing as you add it, continually checking for lumps and even-ness. Hold the legs, body, or whatever part you're working on at arm's length to check for symmetry. For your first attempts you may have to restuff to get it right. Whipstitch the openings closed when you are satisfied with your work.

Just take your time. With a bit of experience you will develop a feel for stuffing and work will progress more quickly.

> *IMPORTANT: When making any doll or doll clothing for a young child (four years or younger), do not use buttons, snaps, pompons, beads, or other decorations that could be pulled or twisted off and swallowed.*

♥

16½"
Character Doll

Create a fairyland full of characters with this one doll body pattern. I made several dolls from this one pattern and then created outfits for nine fairy tale characters: Little Red Riding Hood, Little Bo Peep, Hansel and Gretel, Goldilocks, Cinderella, Fairy Godmother, the Witch, and Pinocchio. With a simple change in the body pattern you can create The Little Mermaid, too!

♥

MATERIALS

¹/₃ yard muslin

Matching thread

Polyester fiberfill stuffing

Permanent marker (see the Basics and Sources)

Acrylic craft paints or embroidery floss: blue, green or brown, black, and red

Fray Check™

Instructions for the generic doll appear first below, followed by instructions for each of the dolls, including hair directions. The Little Mermaid is the only exception. You will find complete instructions for her on page 110.

INSTRUCTIONS

Prepare the patterns and cut, mark, and dye (if desired) the fabric as instructed in the Basics.

Note: A short machine stitch of 1.5 or 8-10 stitches to the inch will make stronger seams and ease stitching around tight curves.

Note: Seam allowances for all body patterns in this book are not included on the pattern pieces. You will stitch on the traced lines and cut the pieces out after stitching. This affords greater accuracy in constructing the dolls.

1. Fold the muslin in half. Lay the body, arm, and leg patterns on the muslin and trace around them leaving an inch or more

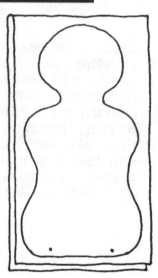

between them. Make one body, two arms, and two legs. Cut them out, leaving a half inch or more outside of the traced lines.

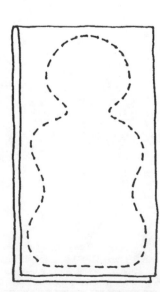

Sew all around the edges of the body, leaving a gap in the stitching between the dots at the bottom of the body for turning and stuffing.

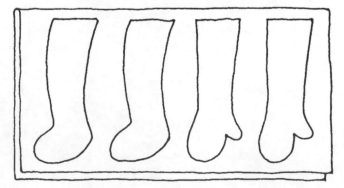

2. Stitch the legs and arms, leaving the top straight edges unstitched.

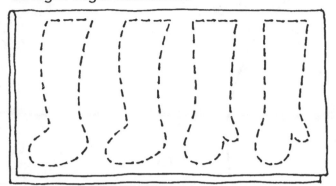

3. Trim all seam allowances to ⅛." Clip seam allowances to stitching at neck, ankle, and thumb as shown. Apply Fray Check™ to these points.

Turn all the body parts right side out.

4. Stuff the head and body. Ladder stitch the opening at the bottom of the body closed.

Stuff the arms to about 4" from the tips of the fingers. Topstitch across the arm as illustrated. Try a zipper foot for this.

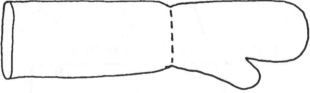

Stuff the legs and arms to within ¾" of the raw edges. Turn ¼" at the raw edges to the inside.

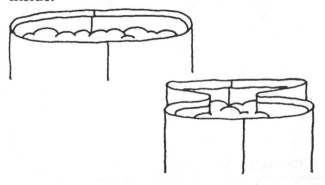

Fold and whipstitch to the body as shown.

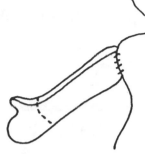

5. To transfer the face pattern to the doll: Trace or copy the face pattern onto a piece of paper. Include the outline of the head, neck, and shoulder. Cut along the outline of the head. Darken the face pattern you copied from the book with a pencil. Lay the penciled side of the paper over the doll's head, lining up the edge of the paper with the seam lines of the head. Hold in place. Rub the back of the face pattern with a blunt object or your thumbnail. Remove the paper.

To paint the face: Go over the lines with the permanent pen. Though this may seem formidable at first, painting is simply a matter of layering. Try a few sample eyes on scrap fabric. Paint the whites of the eyes white. Allow to dry. Paint the eyeballs blue, brown, or green. Let dry. Mix a little white paint with the eye color. Add some faint streaks in the eyes radiating from the center. You may also mix yellow with the eye color paint and add streaks to the eyes. Let dry. Paint black circles at the centers of the eyes. Let dry. Add a small white dot for a highlight to the black iris. For Pinocchio, don't paint the nose. A fabric nose will be sewn to the face.

To embroider the face: Go over the traced face pattern with a pencil. Using three strands of embroidery floss, form eyebrows and nose with backstitches. Embroider eyes with satin stitches. Fill in the mouth with satin stitches.

To finish the doll: To give your doll a rosy glow, add a bit of blush to her cheeks. Using a cotton ball and a light touch, dab a bit of blush on the doll's cheeks. To soften it, dab off some of the color with a fresh cotton ball.

Transfer the shoe patterns in the same way you did the face. Paint the shoes according to the instructions on the shoe patterns. (Omit for those dolls having separately made shoes.)

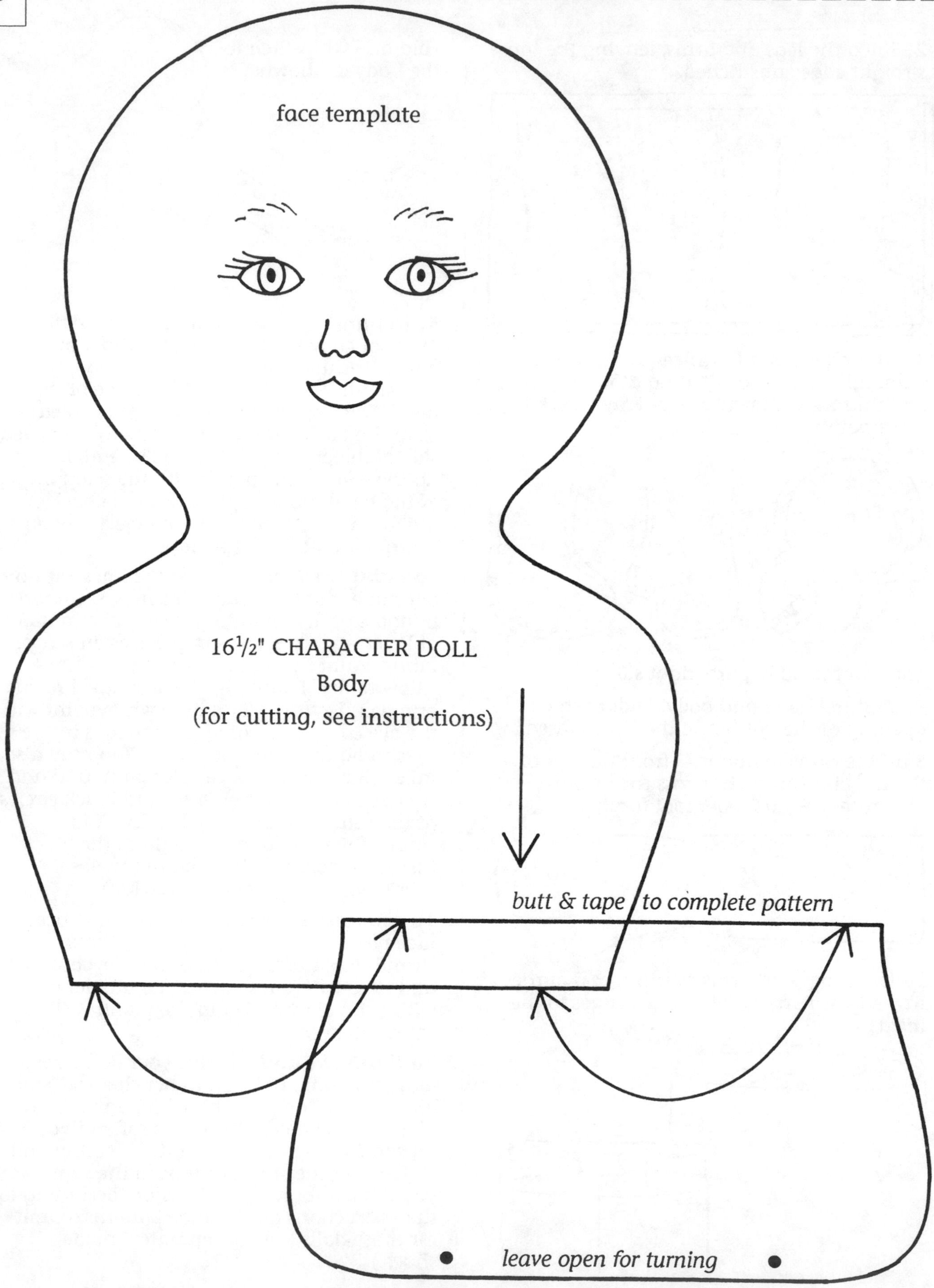

face template

16½" CHARACTER DOLL
Body
(for cutting, see instructions)

butt & tape to complete pattern

leave open for turning

leave open for turning

leave open for turning

16¹/₂"
CHARACTER DOLL
Arm
(for cutting,
see instructions)

16¹/₂" CHARACTER DOLL
Leg
(for cutting, see instructions)

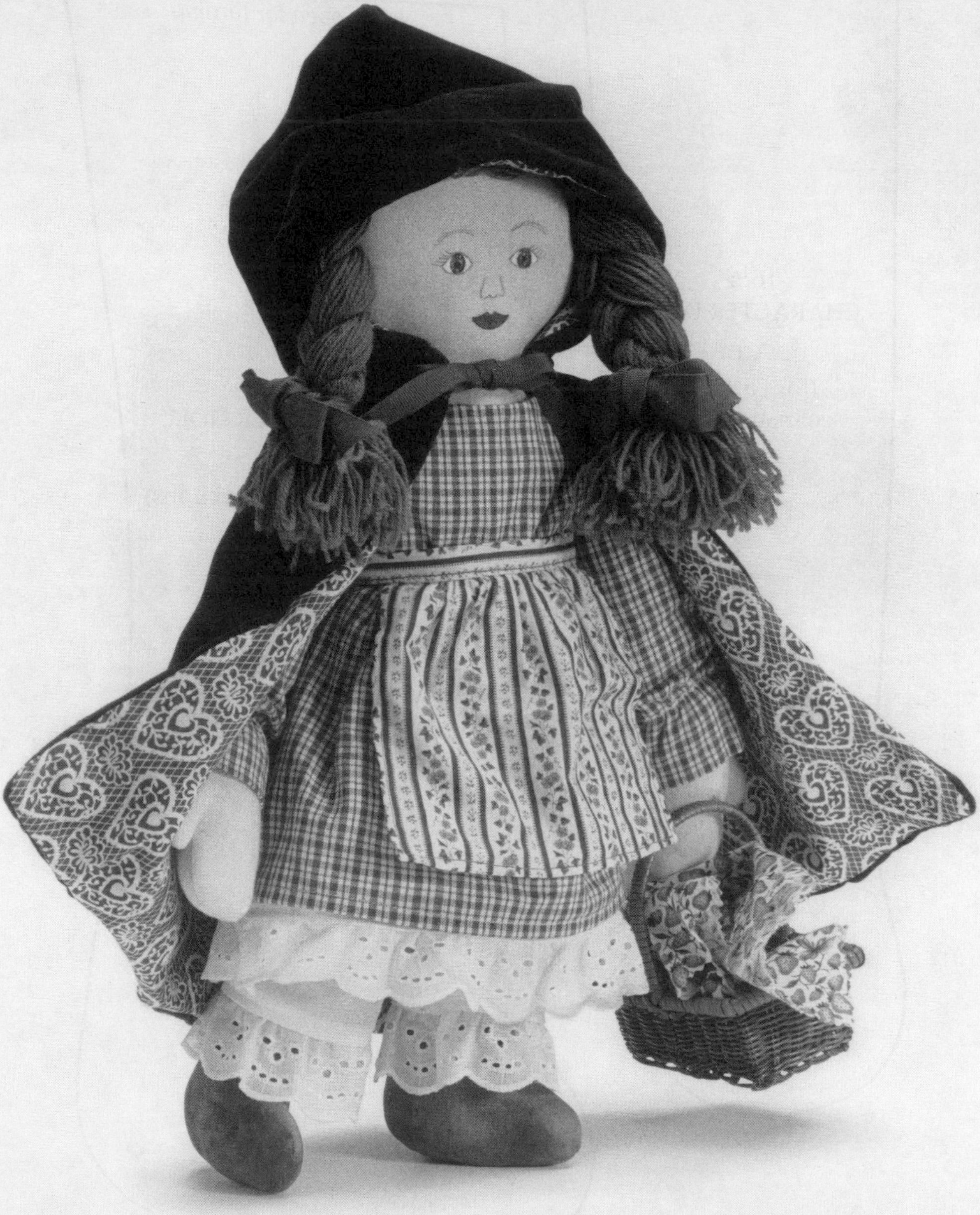

♥

Little Red Riding Hood

Skipping merrily along the path to Grandmother's house, innocent Little Red Riding Hood is totally unaware of the danger awaiting her. To ensure a happy ending, banish all wolves before inviting this beautiful doll inside!

♥

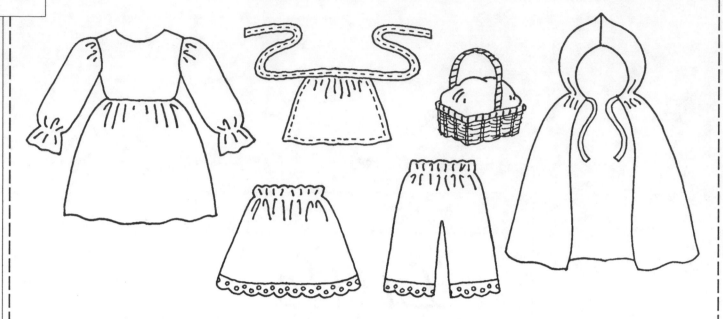

MATERIALS

One skein yarn for hair
(I used Phildars Preface 31R101)

Matching thread

1/3 yard dress fabric

Matching thread

Two 1/4" buttons for dress

1/4 yard apron fabric

Matching thread

3/8 yard red velvet for cape

3/8 yard matching fabric for cape lining

Matching thread

1/3 yard 3/8"-wide red ribbon for cape ties

1 1/4 yards 1"-wide red ribbon for hair ties

1/3 yard white or natural cotton fabric for petticoat and drawers

1 1/8 yards 1 1/2"-wide gathered eyelet for petticoat and drawers

1/2 yard 1/4"-wide elastic

Six 1/4" or 3/8" black shank buttons for shoes

Small basket

INSTRUCTIONS

Turn to page 16 for body instructions. When you have made the doll, painted or embroidered the face, and painted on the shoes, return here and continue to dress the doll and add the hair.

Prepare the patterns and cut and mark the fabric as instructed in the Basics. Cut dress skirt 6 1/4" x 22". Cut petticoat 7" x 22". Cut apron 5 1/2" x 7". Cut one apron tie 1 1/2" x 24".

Note: All seam allowances for clothing are 1/4" and are included in the pattern pieces.

Dress

1. Right sides facing, stitch two front bodice pieces to one back bodice piece at shoulders. Repeat for second set; one will be the bodice, one the lining.

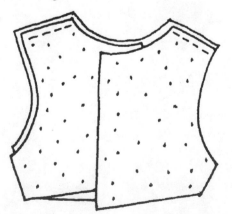

2. Pin bodice to bodice lining along neck edge and center backs, matching shoulder seams. Stitch. Clip curves. Trim corners. Turn.

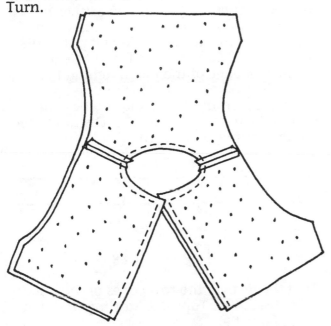

3. Turn the bottom edges of the sleeves 1¹/₂" to the wrong side. Cut two pieces of elastic, each 4" long. Lay the elastic over the raw edge on the wrong side of the sleeve. Place elastic over the raw edge, having the ends of the elastic even with the side edges of the sleeve. Pin the ends in place. Zigzag stitch the elastic in place, along the raw edge of the turned up bottom edge of the sleeve, holding the ends of the elastic firmly and stretching the elastic as you sew. Repeat for second sleeve.

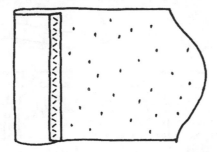

4. Using a long machine stitch, gather the top edge of the sleeve between the dots. Match and pin dots to dots on bodice, treating bodice and bodice lining as one. Pull up on gather stitches. Even out the fullness between the dots and pin. Stitch through sleeve, bodice, and bodice lining. Repeat for other sleeve.

5. Right sides together, sew the underarm and side seams as one.

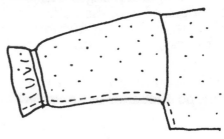

6. Match and pin the two short sides of the dress skirt, right sides facing. Using a ¹/₂" seam allowance, stitch center back seam of dress skirt. Start with a basting stitch, sew half way down the center back seam of the dress skirt. Change to a regular sewing stitch. Backstitch a few stitches. Sew to the bottom edge of the skirt. Backstitch.

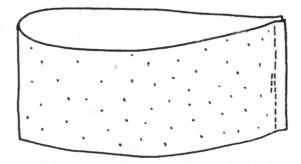

Press the seam open. Turn under ¹/₄" on each seam allowance. For the hem, press under ¹/₄" on the skirt bottom (remember that the basting stitches are at the top end of the skirt) and then another ¹/₄". Starting at the one side of the top of the center back seam, continuing around the hem of the skirt and up the other side of the center back seam of the skirt, topstitch. Remove basting stitches.

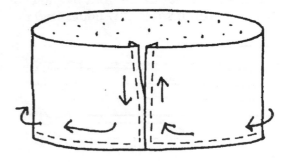

7. Using two rows of gathering stitches, gather the top edge of the skirt starting 1½" from the center back opening edges. Pin the skirt to the bottom edge of the bodice (through both layers), right sides facing, matching center backs. Adjust gathers. Pin. Stitch.

8. Make buttonholes on bodice as marked. Try on doll. Mark positions for buttons. Sew buttons on.

Apron

1. On two short apron edges, press raw edge ¼" to wrong side. Repeat. Do the same for one long edge. Topstitch.

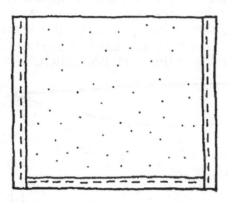

Tip: Often when I turn the corner with my needle in the fabric and try to continue stitching along the next edge I find the fabric gets bunched up. Try placing the apron on a piece of tear-away stabilizer. Then stitch as normal. Simply tear the stabilizer away after stitching. So much easier!

2. Using two rows of a long machine stitch, gather the remaining raw edge of the apron.

3. Press the apron tie in half lengthwise. Open the fold up again and turn the long raw edges in to meet at the fold in the center. Press. Turn the short raw edges in ¼".

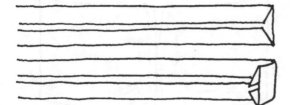

4. Unfold the tie. Find the center of the tie. Place a pin 1" to one side of this point. (This will make the tie lengths uneven. When you tie the apron on the doll you won't find that one tie is much longer than the other.) Measure 1⅞" to each side of the first pin. Mark with pins. Remove the first pin. Right sides facing, pin the raw edge of the apron to one raw edge of the tie, matching the apron side edges to the pins on the apron tie. Pull up on the gathering stitches and gather the apron to fit the tie. Distribute the gathers evenly. Pin. Stitch.

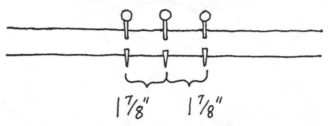

Fold the tie over the raw edges of the apron as pressed. Pin. Topstitch starting at the far end of one tie.

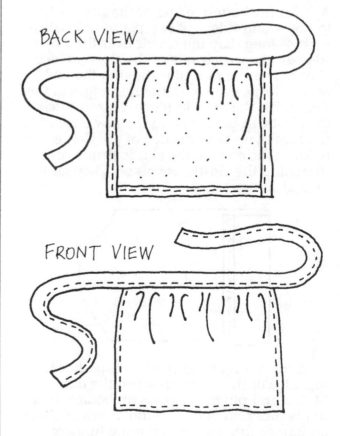

BACK VIEW

FRONT VIEW

Drawers

1. Fold one drawer piece in half the same way you cut it out. Stitch the inside leg seam. Repeat for the other drawer piece.

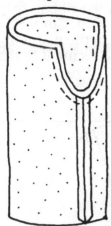 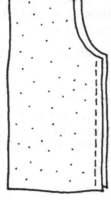

2. Turn one drawer piece right side out. Put it inside the other drawer piece, which is still wrong side out (right sides are thus facing). Match the long curved crotch seam. Stitch.

3. Turn drawer right side out. Press under $1/4$" on the top edge. Press under $1/2$". Topstitch along the bottom fold, leaving a $1/2$" or so wide gap in the stitching for inserting elastic.

4. Cut a piece of elastic 9" long. Attach a safety pin to each end. Insert one safety pin into the casing. Work it all the way around and push it back out the opening. Overlap the ends of the elastic $1/2$". Stitch them together.

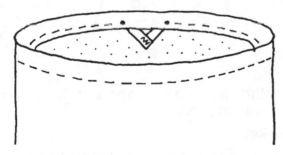

5. Press under $1/4$" on the bottom edge of the drawers legs. Press under another $1/4$".

Cut two pieces of eyelet, each 8" long. Seam the two short edges of one piece together. Repeat for the second piece. Right side of eyelet facing wrong side of drawer leg, pin the top band of the eyelet to the turned under hem of the drawer leg. Stitch as shown.

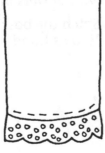

Petticoat

1. Press under $1/4$" on one long edge (making it the bottom edge) of the petticoat. Press under another $1/4$".

Cut one piece of eyelet 22" long. Right side of eyelet facing wrong side of petticoat, pin the top band of the eyelet to the turned under hem of the petticoat. Stitch as shown.

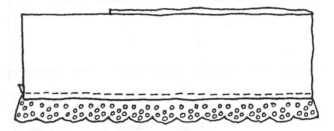

2. Fold the petticoat in half as shown. Stitch the short center back seam, including the eyelet.

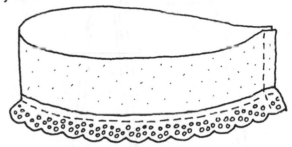

3. Press under $1/4$" on the remaining long edge (the top edge). Press under $1/2$". Topstitch along the bottom fold, leaving a $1/2$" or so wide opening for inserting elastic.

4. Cut a piece of elastic 9" long. Attach a safety pin to each end. Insert one safety pin into the casing. Work it all the way around and push it back out the opening. Overlap the ends of the elastic $1/2$". Stitch them together.

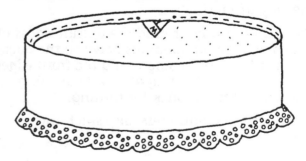

Cape

1. Right sides facing, stitch the two velvet cape pieces together as shown.

Repeat for the two cape lining pieces.

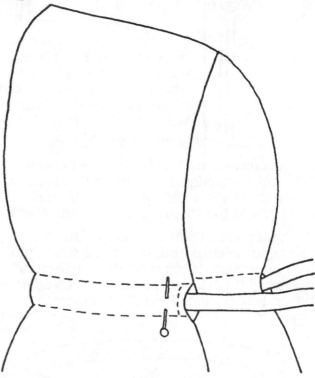

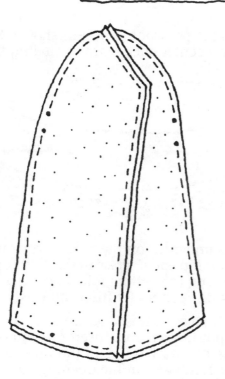

2. Right sides facing, pin the velvet cape to the cape lining, matching the raw edges all the way around.

Stitch all the way around the outside edges of the cape, leaving openings between the dots for the ribbon tie casing along the front edges of the cape and leaving a 3"-wide opening at the center bottom back for turning.

Turn right side out. Press. Slip stitch the opening closed.

3. Topstitch along the ribbon casing lines marked on the lining through the lining and the velvet.

Attach a safety pin to one end of the ribbon. Insert the ribbon into the casing. Leave about eight inches of ribbon extending from one opening in the cape. Pin the ribbon to secure it. Put the cape on the doll. Gather the cape onto the ribbon to fit it to the doll. Pin the other end of the ribbon to secure it to the cape.

Topstitch through the cape and the ribbon to secure in place.

Basket

Pink the edges of a piece of Little Red Riding Hood's leftover dress or apron fabric appropriately sized for her basket. Fill the basket with flowers or fabric.

Stitch the basket into Little Red Riding Hood's hand.

Hair

1. Cut the yarn into 28" lengths.

2. Draw a line on a piece of paper 4" long. Place the paper so the top of the line is under the presser foot of your sewing machine. Find the center of the bundle of the 28"-long yarn. Lay it centered on the paper over the drawn line. Stitch the yarn to the paper, evening out the yarn along the line. This will be the part.

Tear one side of the paper from the stitching and then the other.

Cut the hair ribbon into two pieces.

Starting at the doll's forehead, place the "part" of the wig on the doll. Stitch the seam over the top of the head and continue straight down the center back of the head. Braid each side of the hair as far as you can and tie them with an extra piece of yarn. Trim the uneven ends of the braids evenly. Tie each with one half of the hair ribbon. Trim the ribbon.

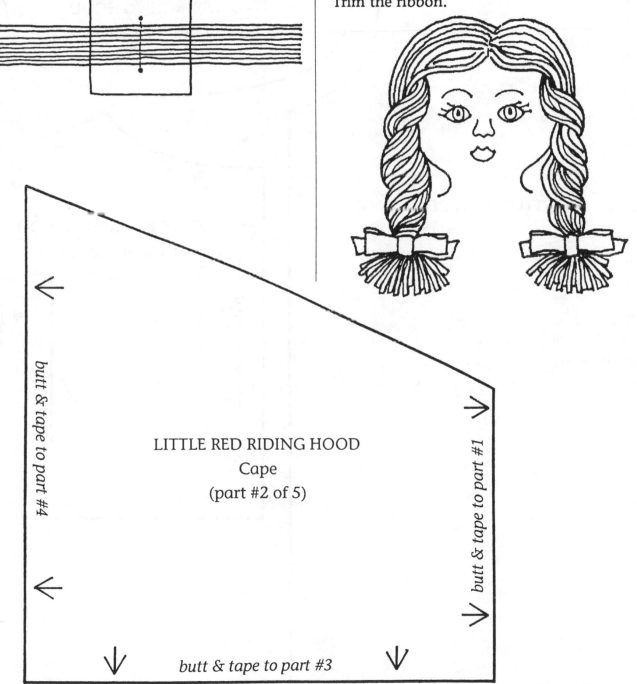

LITTLE RED RIDING HOOD
Cape
(part #2 of 5)

butt & tape to part #4

butt & tape to part #1

butt & tape to part #3

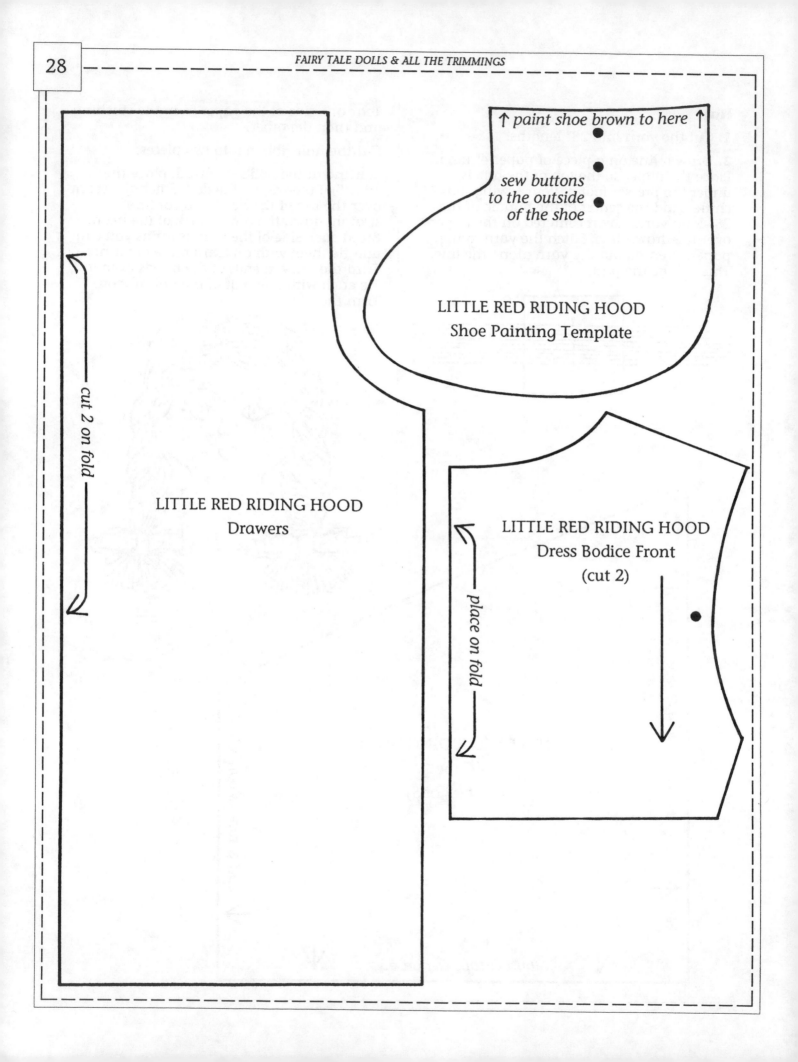

↑ paint shoe brown to here ↑

sew buttons to the outside of the shoe

LITTLE RED RIDING HOOD
Shoe Painting Template

cut 2 on fold

LITTLE RED RIDING HOOD
Drawers

place on fold

LITTLE RED RIDING HOOD
Dress Bodice Front
(cut 2)

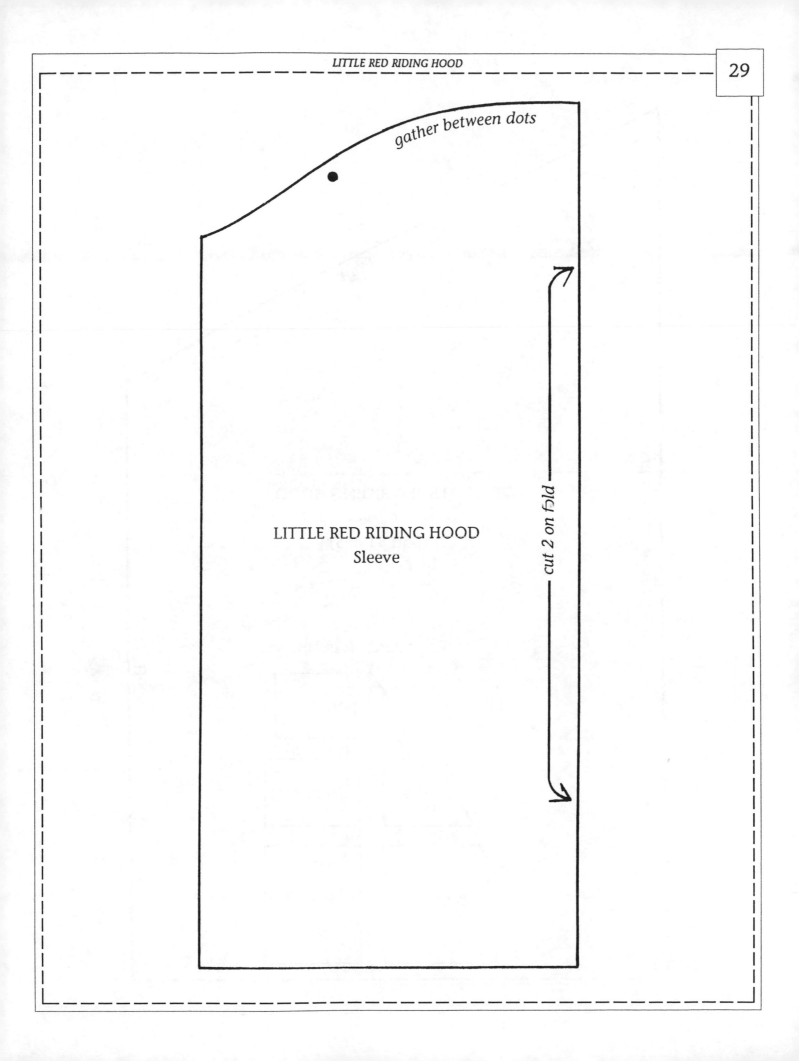

gather between dots

LITTLE RED RIDING HOOD
Sleeve

cut 2 on fold

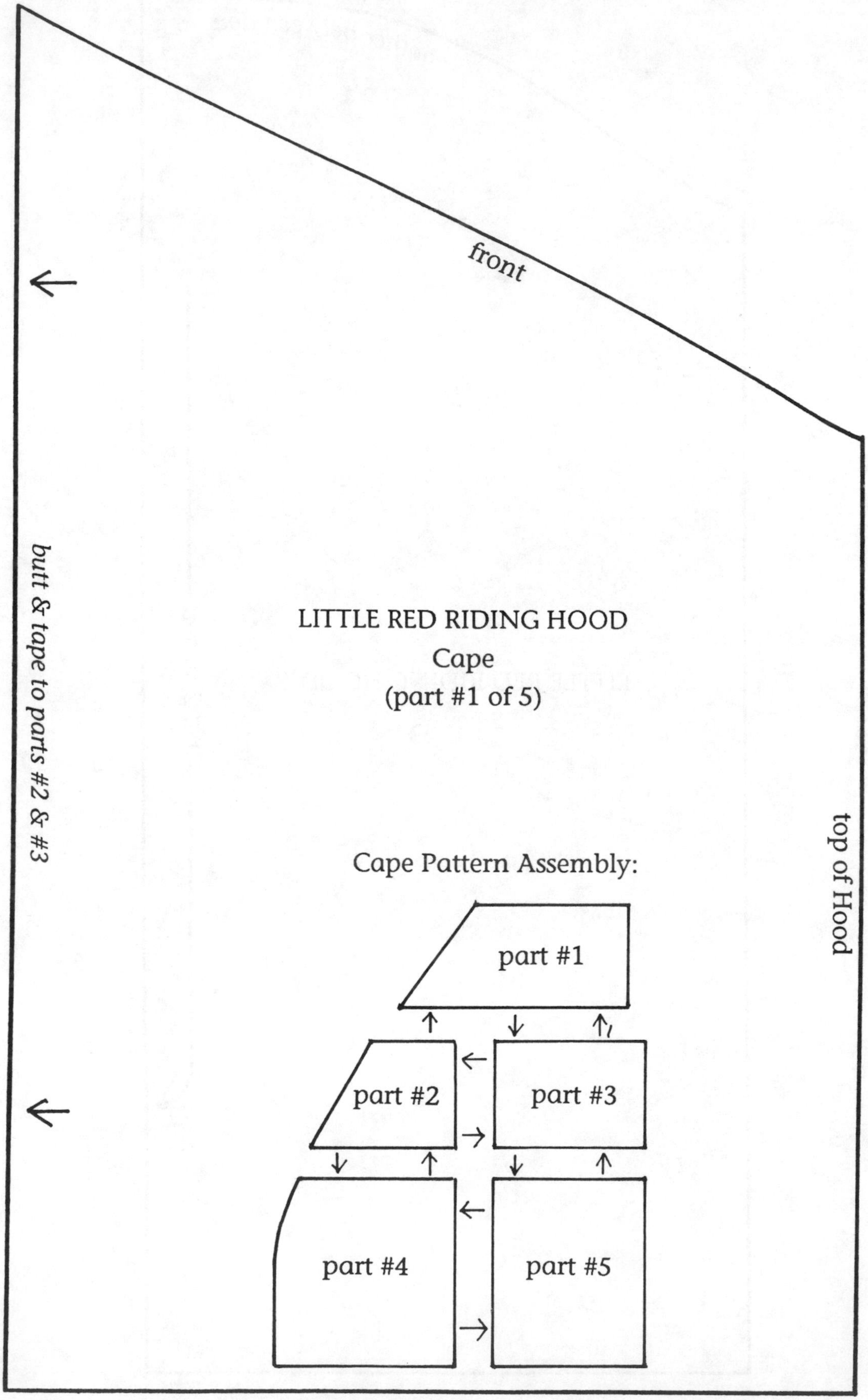

← front

← butt & tape to parts #2 & #3

top of Hood

LITTLE RED RIDING HOOD
Cape
(part #1 of 5)

Cape Pattern Assembly:

part #1

part #2   part #3

part #4   part #5

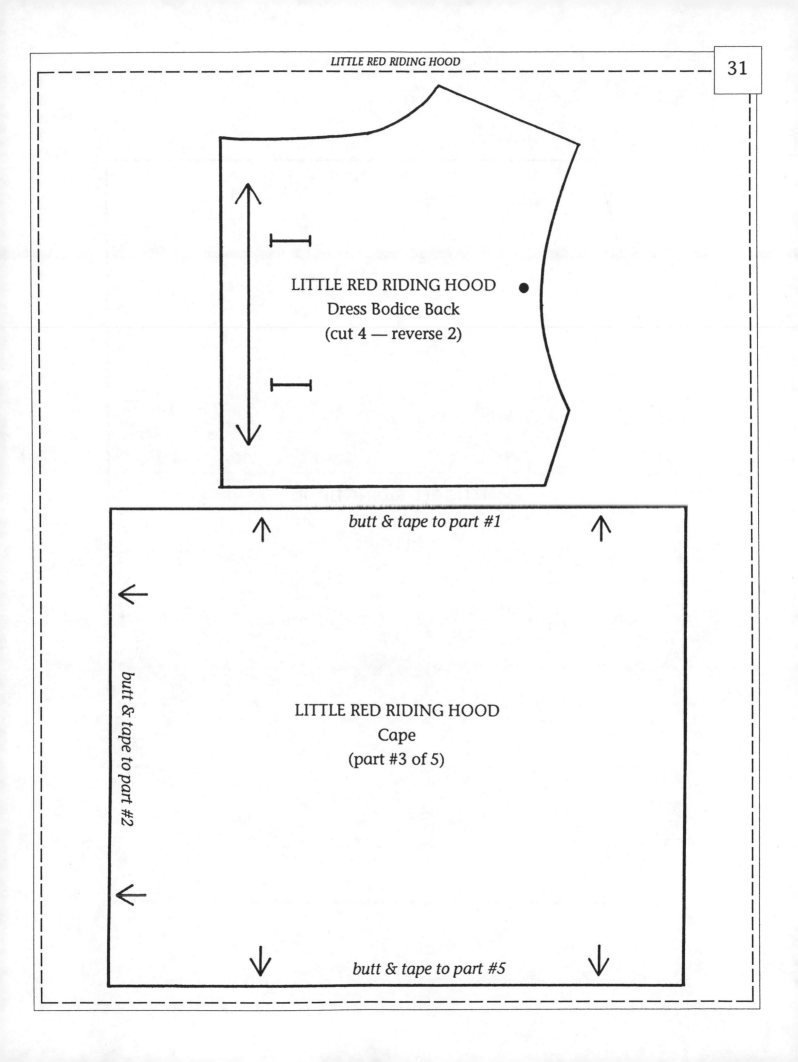

LITTLE RED RIDING HOOD
Dress Bodice Back
(cut 4 — reverse 2)

butt & tape to part #1

butt & tape to part #2

LITTLE RED RIDING HOOD
Cape
(part #3 of 5)

butt & tape to part #5

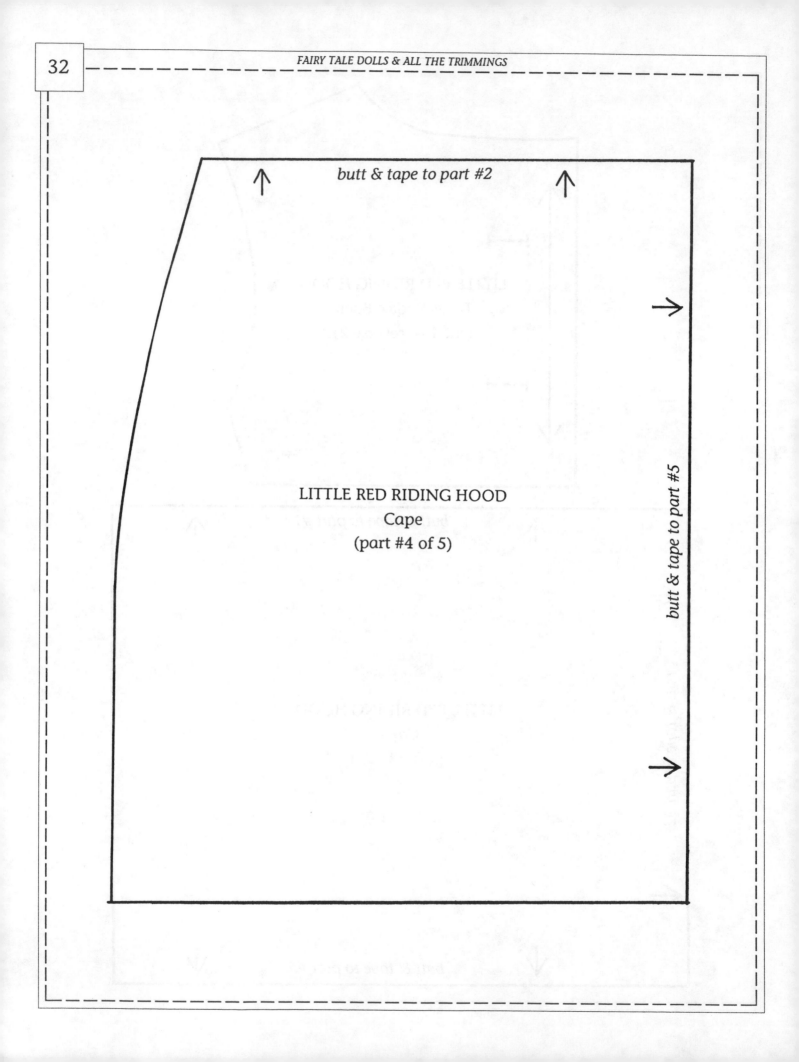

butt & tape to part #2

LITTLE RED RIDING HOOD
Cape
(part #4 of 5)

butt & tape to part #5

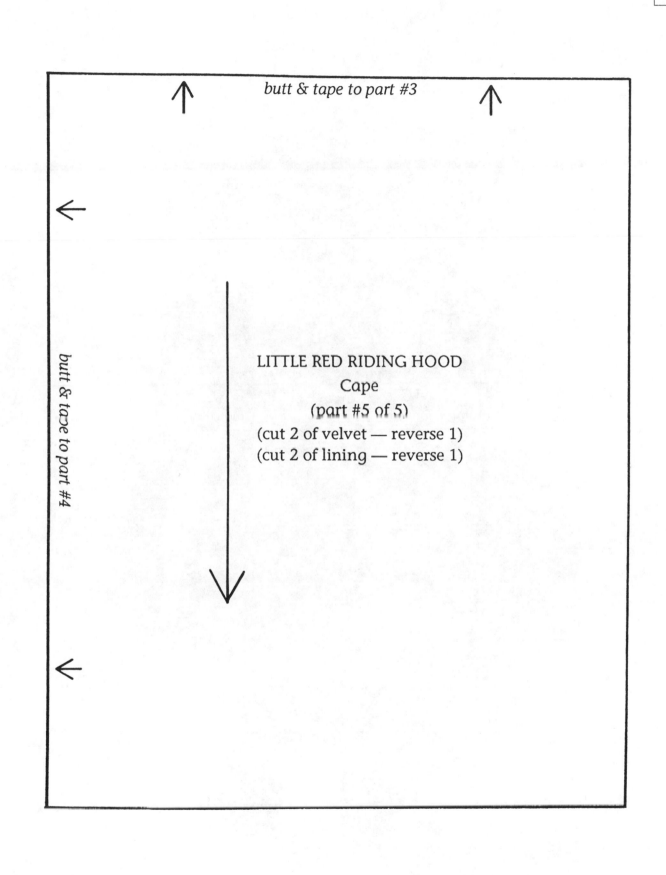

butt & tape to part #3

butt & tape to part #4

LITTLE RED RIDING HOOD
Cape
(part #5 of 5)
(cut 2 of velvet — reverse 1)
(cut 2 of lining — reverse 1)

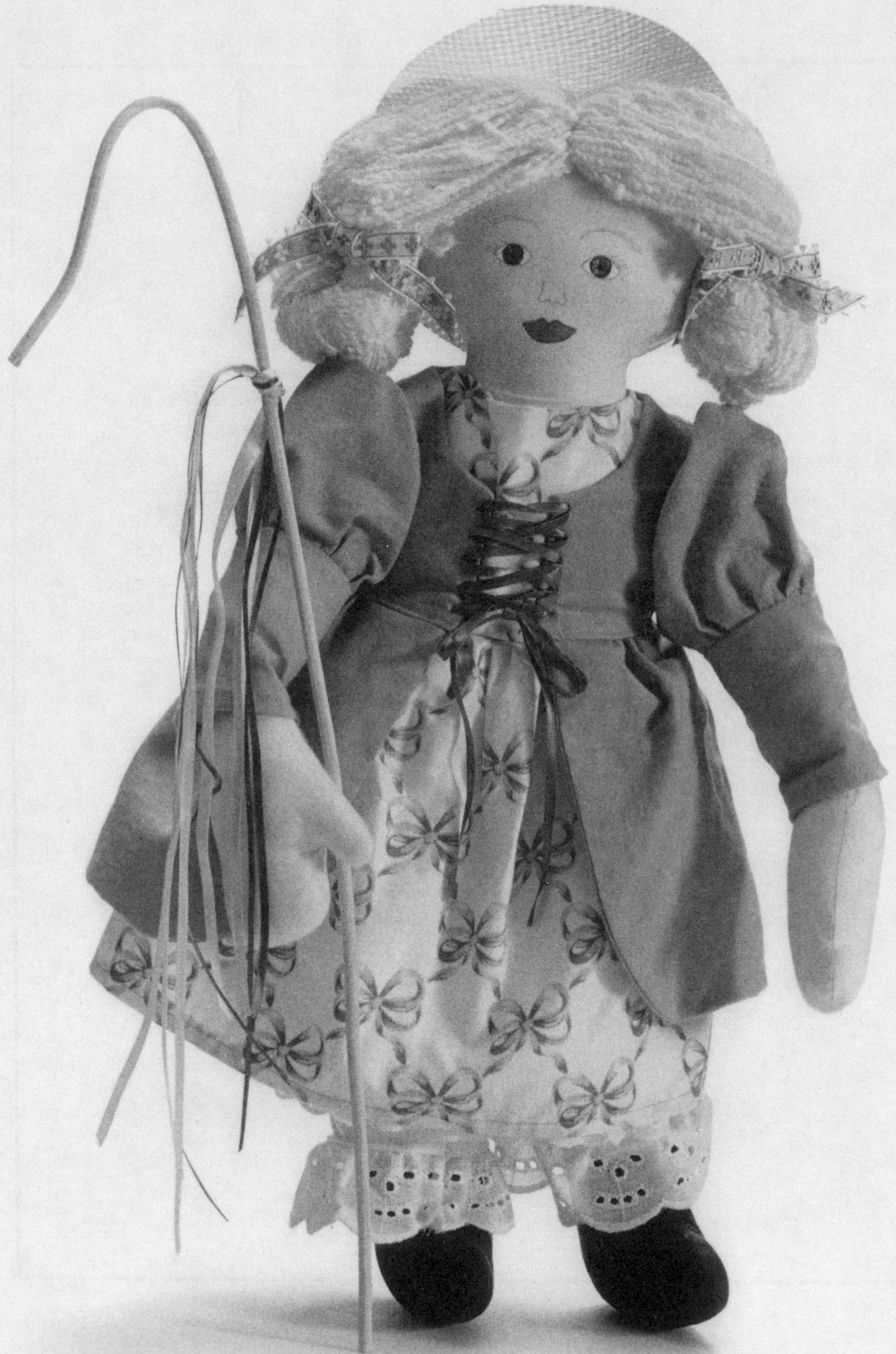

♥

Little Bo Peep

Clothed in a jacket and dress, a bonnet atop her head, and a staff in her hand, Little Bo Peep is well-prepared to tend her flock. This little lady is sure to please adults and children alike.

♥

MATERIALS

1 skein yarn (I used Cotton Candy shade 2903 by Brunswick)

Fabric stiffener

1/3 yard dress fabric

Matching thread

Two 1/4" buttons for the dress

1/3 yard overdress fabric

Matching thread

1 yard 1/8"-wide ribbon for overdress bodice fastening ties

1/3 yard white or natural cotton fabric for petticoat and drawers

1 1/8 yards 1 1/2"-wide gathered eyelet for petticoat and drawers

1/2 yard 1/4"-wide elastic

Six 1/4" or 3/8" black shank buttons for shoes

White bonnet (see Sources)

1 1/4 yard ribbon for hair ties and to trim bonnet

18"-long piece of 1/4"-wide (or so) round basket making reed for staff

Scraps of ribbons to adorn staff

White acrylic paint to decorate staff

INSTRUCTIONS

Turn to page 16 for body instructions. When you have made the doll, painted or embroidered the face, and painted on the shoes, return here and continue to dress the doll and add the hair.

Prepare the patterns and cut and mark the fabric as instructed in the Basics. Cut dress skirt 7 1/2" x 22". Cut petticoat 7" x 22".

Note: All seam allowances for clothing are 1/4" and are included in the pattern pieces.

Dress

1. Right sides facing, stitch two front bodice pieces to one back bodice piece at shoulders. Repeat for second set; one will be the bodice, one the lining.

2. Pin bodice to bodice lining along neck edge and center backs, matching shoulder seams. Stitch. Clip curves. Trim corners. Turn.

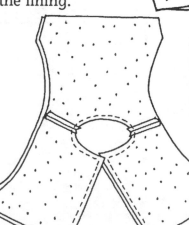

3. Press ¼" on the bottom edge of the sleeves to the wrong side. Repeat. Topstitch.

4. Using a long machine stitch, gather the top edge of the sleeve between the dots. Match and pin dots to dots on bodice, treating bodice and bodice lining as one. Pull up on gather stitches. Even out the fullness between the dots and pin. Stitch through sleeve, bodice, and bodice lining. Repeat for other sleeve.

5. Right sides together, sew the underarm and side seams as one.

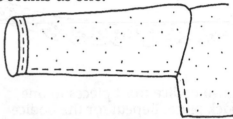

6. Match and pin the two short sides of the dress skirt, right sides facing. Using a ½-inch seam allowance, stitch center back seam of dress skirt. Start with a basting stitch, sew half way down the center back seam of the dress skirt. Change to a regular sewing stitch. Backstitch a few stitches. Sew to the bottom edge of the skirt. Backstitch.

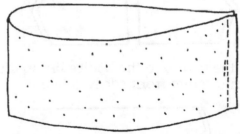

Press the seam open. Turn under ¼" on each seam allowance. For the hem, press under ¼" on the skirt bottom (remember that the basting stitches are at the top end of the skirt) and then another ¼". Starting at one side of the top of the center back seam, continuing around the hem of the skirt and up the other side of the center back seam of the skirt, topstitch. Remove basting stitches.

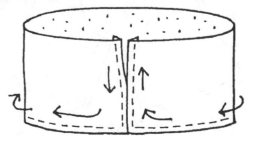

7. Using two rows of gathering stitches, gather the top edge of the skirt starting 1½" from the center back opening edges. Pin the skirt to the bottom edge of the bodice (through both layers), right sides facing, matching center backs. Adjust gathers. Pin. Stitch.

8. Make buttonholes on bodice as marked. Try on doll. Mark positions for buttons. Sew buttons on.

Drawers

1. Fold one drawer piece in half the same way you cut it out, right sides facing. Stitch the inside leg seam. Repeat for the other drawer piece.

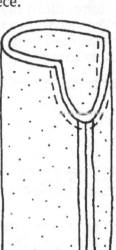

2. Turn one drawer piece right side out. Put it inside the other drawer piece, which is still wrong side out (right sides are thus facing). Match the long, curved crotch seam. Stitch.

3. Turn drawers right side out. Press under ¼" on the top edge. Press under ½". Topstitch along the bottom fold, leaving a ½"-wide gap in the stitching for inserting elastic.

4. Cut a piece of elastic 9" long. Attach a safety pin to each end. Insert one safety pin into the casing. Work it all the way around and push it back out the opening. Overlap the ends of the elastic ½". Stitch them together.

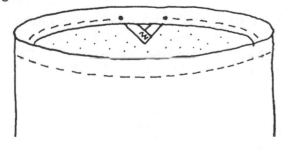

5. Press under ¼" on the bottom edge of the drawer legs. Press under another ¼".

Cut two pieces of eyelet, each 8" long. Seam the two short edges of one piece together. Repeat for the second piece. Right side of eyelet facing wrong side of drawer leg, pin the top band of the eyelet to the turned under hem of the drawer leg. Stitch as shown.

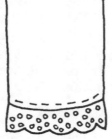

Petticoat

1. Press under ¼" on one long edge (making it the bottom edge) of the petticoat. Press under another ¼".

Cut one piece of eyelet 22" long. Right side of eyelet facing wrong side of petticoat, pin the top band of the eyelet to the turned under hem of the petticoat. Stitch as shown.

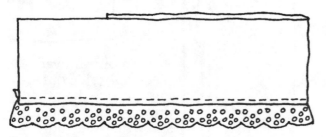

2. Fold the petticoat in half as shown. Stitch the short center back seam, including the eyelet.

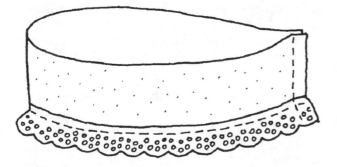

3. Press under ¼" on the remaining long edge (the top edge). Press under ½". Topstitch along the bottom fold, leaving a ½" or so wide opening for inserting elastic.

4. Cut a piece of elastic 9" long. Attach a safety pin to each end. Insert one safety pin into the casing. Work it all the way around and push it back out the opening. Overlap the ends of the elastic ½". Stitch them together.

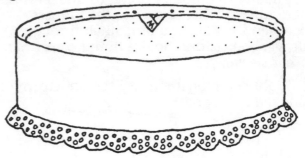

Jacket

1. Stitch two bodice front pieces to one bodice back piece. Repeat for the bodice lining.

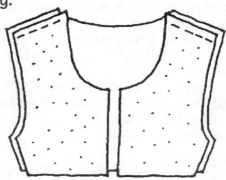

2. Pin the bodice to the bodice lining along neck and center front edges. Stitch.

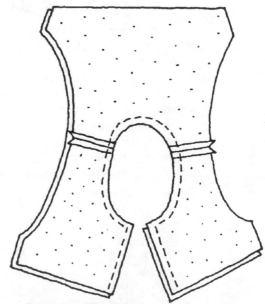

Turn right side out. Press.

3. Gather stitch between dots on long straight edge at bottom of sleeve top. Also gather stitch top curved edge between dots.

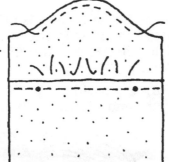

Matching the dots on sleeve top and sleeve bottom, pin the bottom straight edge of the sleeve top to the sleeve bottom, right sides facing. Pull up on gather stitches to fit. Pin. Adjust gather stitches. Pin. Stitch.

From now on, treat the two layers of the bodice as one. Match the dots on the top curved edge of the sleeve top to the dots on the bodice. Pin. Pull up on the gather stitches. Adjust. Pin. Stitch.

4. Stitch the underarm/side seam.

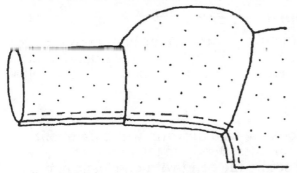

5. Press the bottom edges of the sleeve ¼" to the wrong side. Repeat. Topstitch.

6. Stitch the two overdress skirts together, right sides facing, leaving the top, long straight edges open.

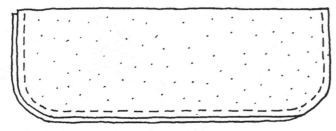

Turn right side out. Press.

7. Using two rows of gathering stitches, gather the top edge of the skirt starting 1" from the center front edges. Pin the skirt to the bottom edge of the bodice (through both layers), right sides facing, matching center fronts. Adjust gathers. Pin. Stitch.

8. Put the overdress on the doll. Starting at the top, sew the ribbon to the bodice front as shown.

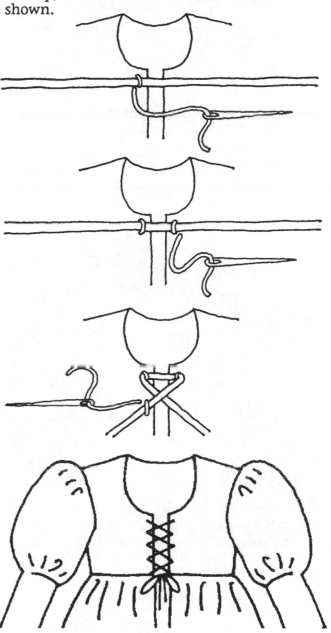

Hair

1. Unroll and cut the yarn into 28" lengths and put them in a neat pile. Reserve a foot or so for tying the braids.

2. Draw a line 4" long on a piece of paper. Put it under your sewing machine presser foot. Move the yarn as one group to the sewing machine. Stitch the yarn to the paper, having the middle of the yarn on the line and filling the length of the line evenly with the yarn. Backstitch at the beginning and ends of the stitching.

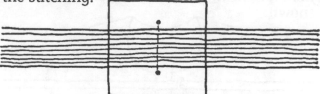

Tear first one side of the paper from the stitching and then the other.

3. Hand stitch the machine stitching to the doll's head as if it were the part of the hair.

4. Cut the reserved yarn into four pieces. Use one piece to tie the first side of the hair into a ponytail and then a second piece of yarn for the other ponytail. The ties are located just below the eyes.

5. Braid the ponytails below these ties for 4". Tie them off with the last two pieces of yarn. Trim the extra ponytail below this bluntly, close to the tie.

Turn the braid up and under, hiding the blunt end. Hand stitch to the head.

Cut the hair tie ribbon into two pieces. Tie them into bows. Stitch them over the braids.

Bonnet

Tie the ribbon around the bonnet so the bow is at the side. Tack or glue the ribbon to the bonnet. Tack or glue the bonnet to the doll's head.

Staff

1. Soak the reed in warm water for about five minutes. Bend the top four inches down and secure the bend with an elastic band. Bend the bottom of this turned down end as shown. Straighten the main shaft of the staff. Set aside to dry.

2. Water down some white acrylic paint to make a wash. Paint the staff. Allow to dry. Tie ribbons around the staff.

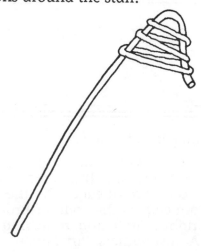

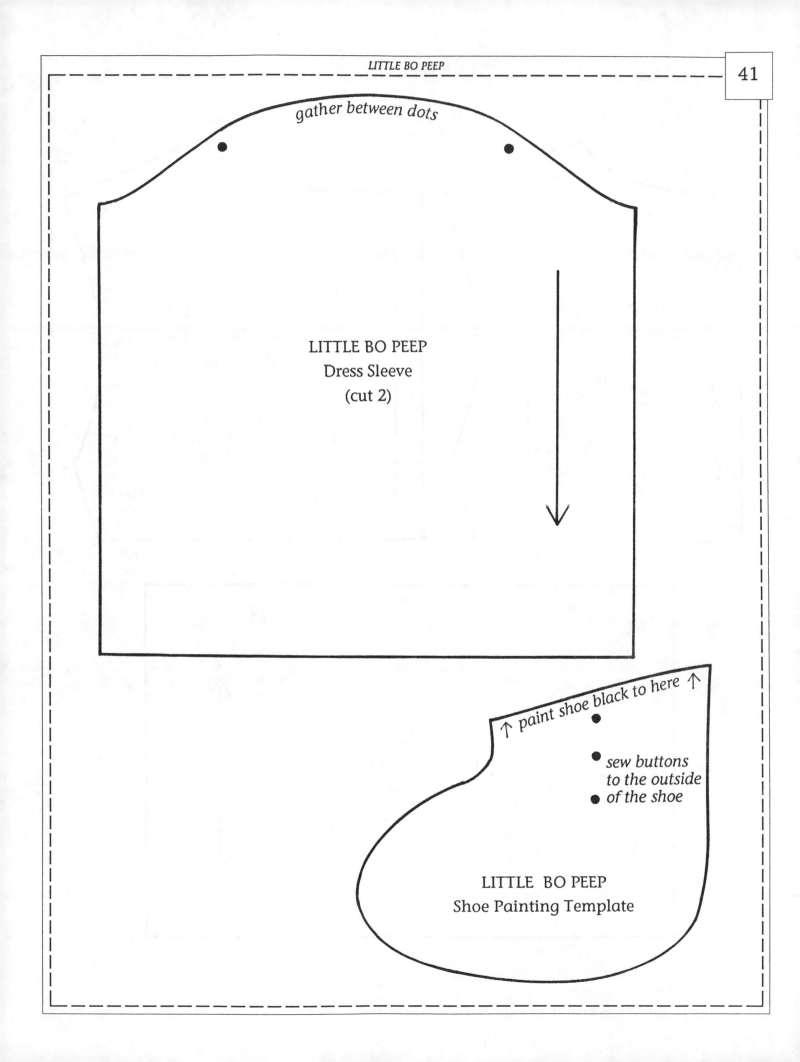

gather between dots

LITTLE BO PEEP
Dress Sleeve
(cut 2)

↑ *paint shoe black to here* ↑

*sew buttons
to the outside
of the shoe*

LITTLE BO PEEP
Shoe Painting Template

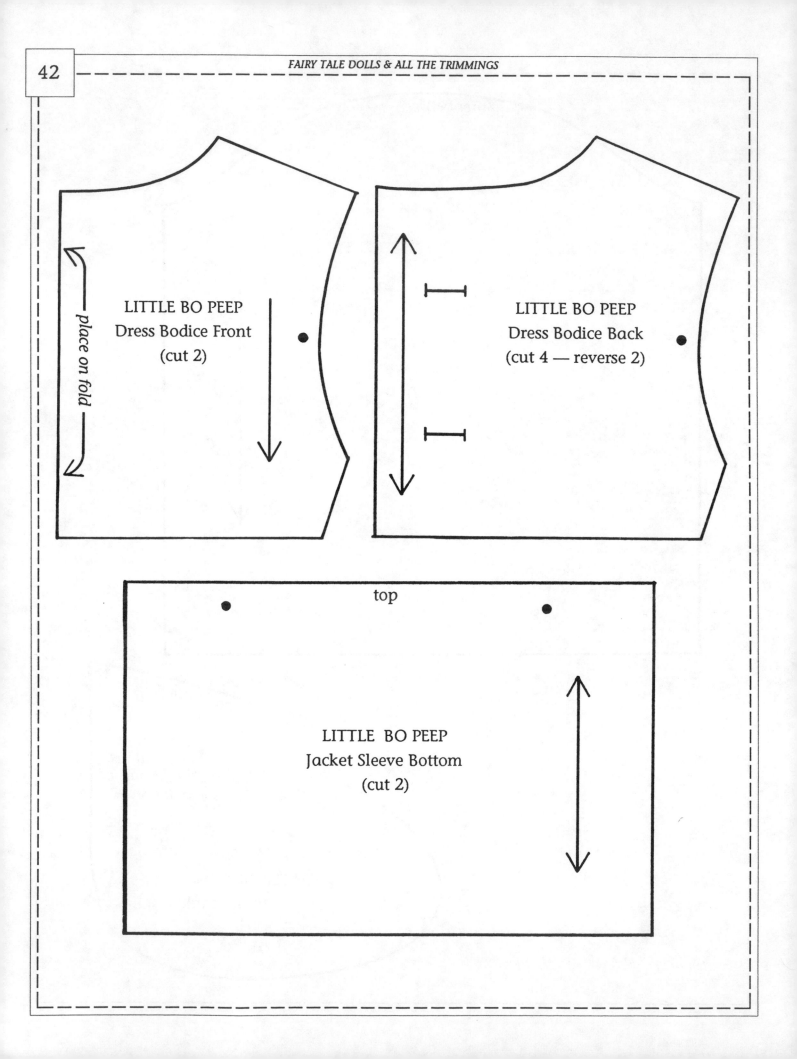

place on fold

LITTLE BO PEEP
Dress Bodice Front
(cut 2)

LITTLE BO PEEP
Dress Bodice Back
(cut 4 — reverse 2)

top

LITTLE BO PEEP
Jacket Sleeve Bottom
(cut 2)

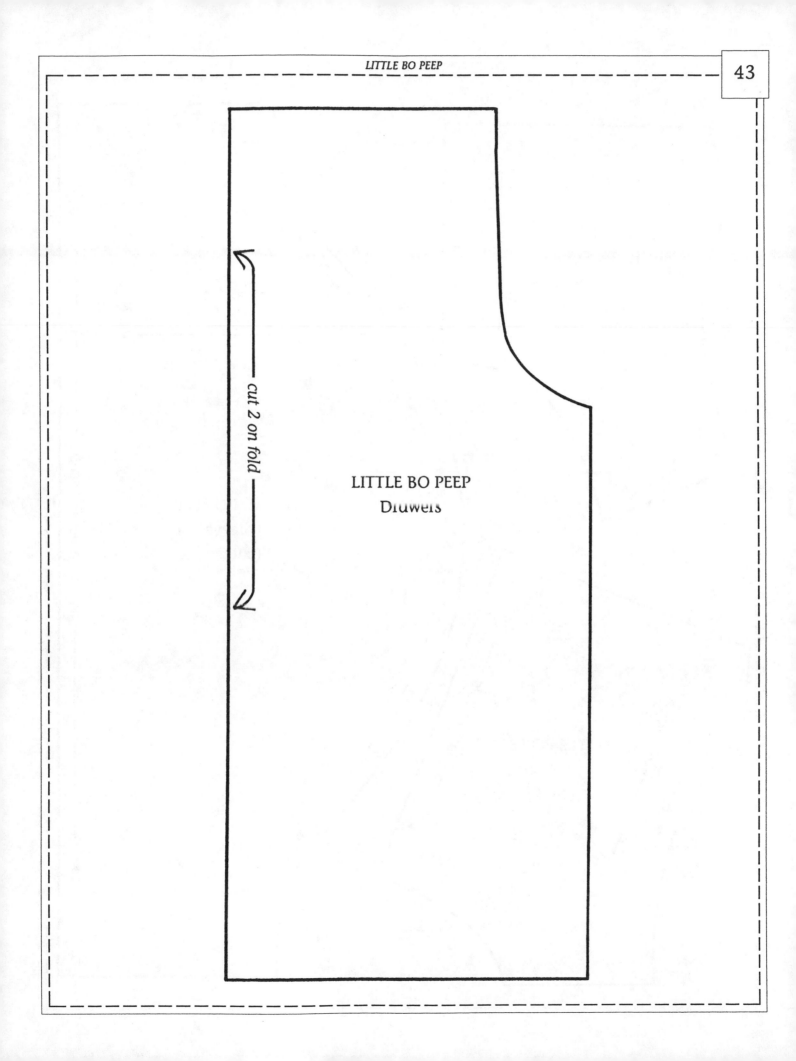

cut 2 on fold

LITTLE BO PEEP
Drawers

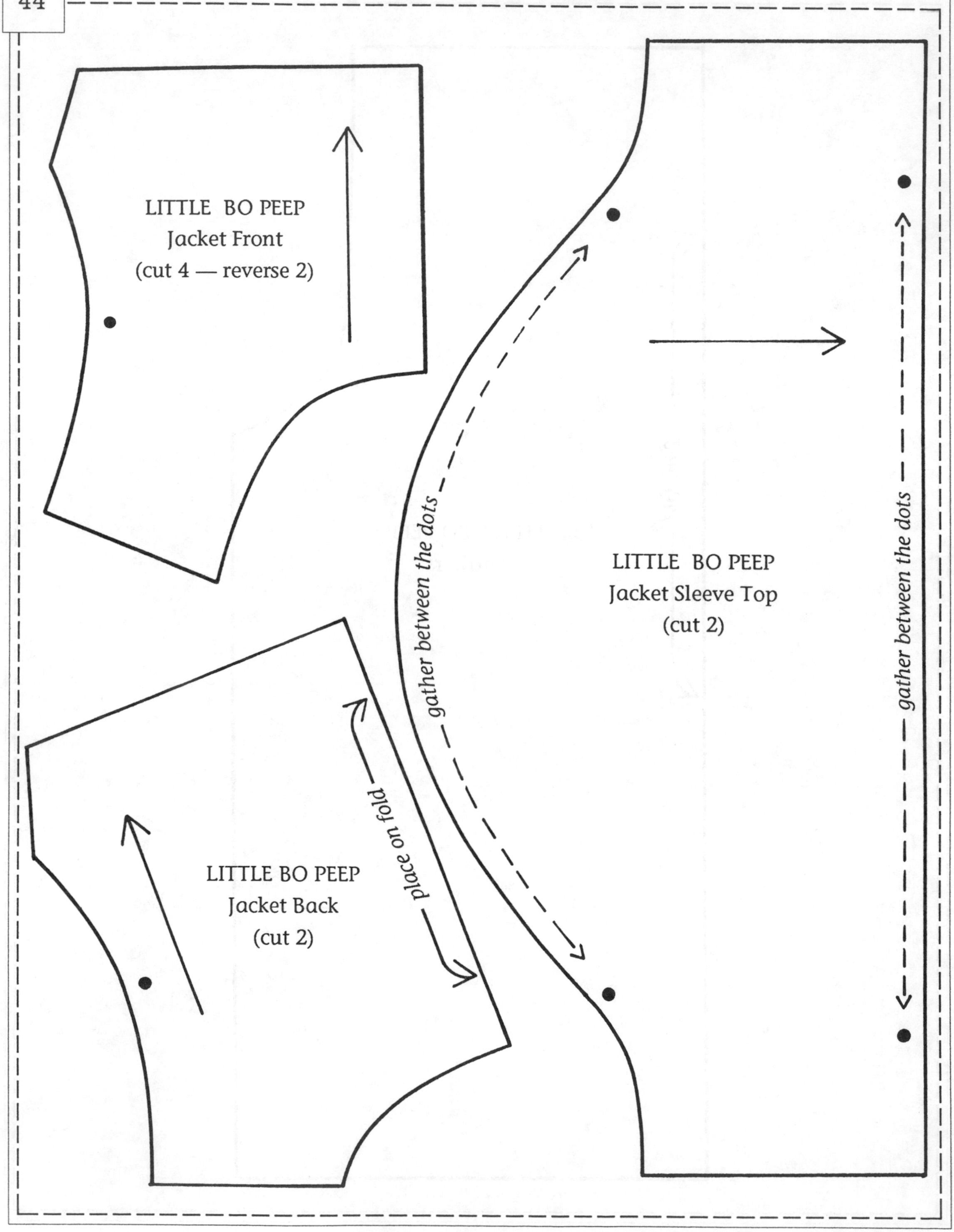

LITTLE BO PEEP
Jacket Front
(cut 4 — reverse 2)

LITTLE BO PEEP
Jacket Sleeve Top
(cut 2)

gather between the dots

gather between the dots

place on fold

LITTLE BO PEEP
Jacket Back
(cut 2)

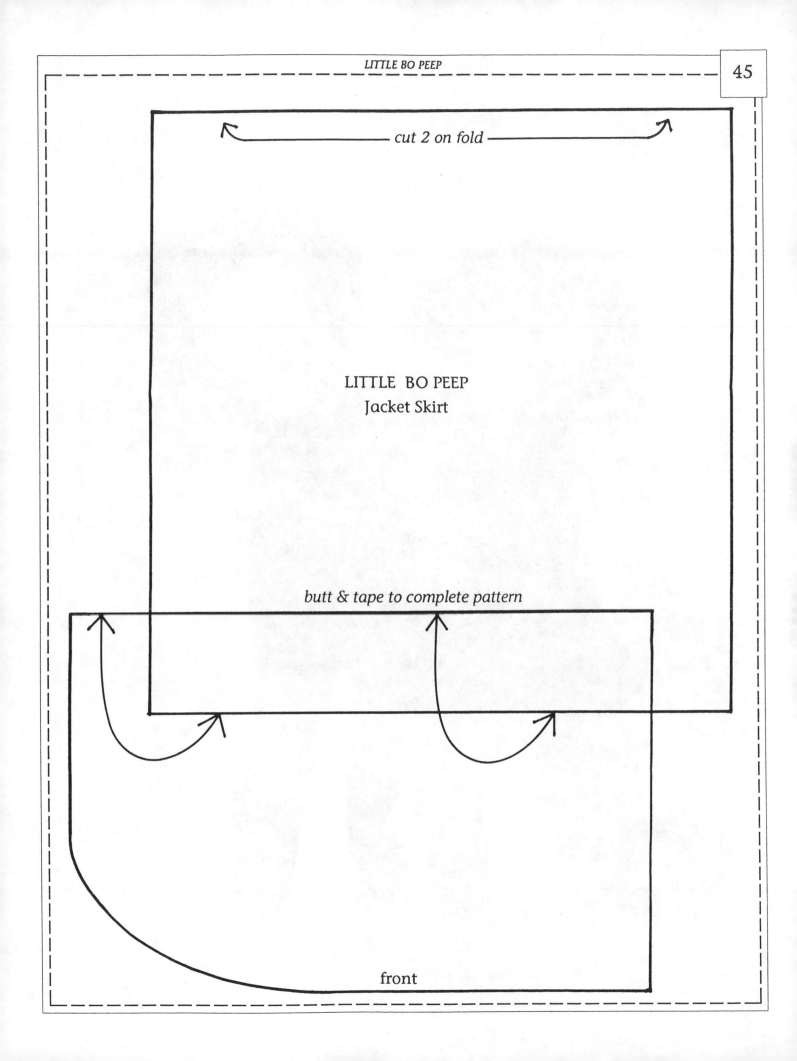

cut 2 on fold

LITTLE BO PEEP
Jacket Skirt

butt & tape to complete pattern

front

♥

Hansel
&
Gretel

Embellish this duo's outfits with colored machine embroidery thread using those lovely built-in stitches in your machine. Or stitch rickrack or woven ribbon to brighten these gingerbread twins' traditional clothing.

♥

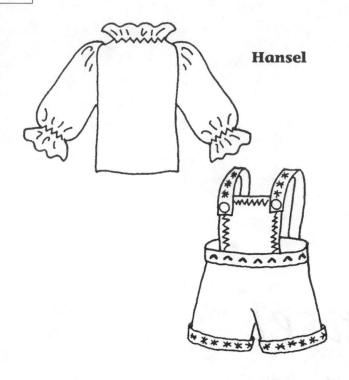

Hansel

MATERIALS

½ skein yarn (I used Cotton Candy shade 2933, gingersnap by Brunswick)
¼ yard white cotton fabric for shirt
Matching thread
½ yard ¼"-wide elastic
¼ yard doe suede, corduroy, wool, or cotton for overalls
Matching thread
Colored embroidery thread or rickrack
Two ½" silver buttons
Six ¼" or ⅜" black shank buttons for shoes

INSTRUCTIONS

Turn to page 16 for body instructions. When you have made the doll, painted or embroidered the face, and painted on the shoes, return here and continue to dress the doll and add the hair.

Prepare the patterns and cut and mark the fabric as instructed in the Basics.

Note: All seam allowances for clothing are ¼" and are included in the pattern pieces.

Shirt

1. Stitch the two shirt pieces together at one shoulder.

2. Press ¾" at neck edge of shirt down to wrong side of shirt. Cut a piece of elastic 6" long. Pin one end of the elastic over the raw edge, having the end of the elastic even with the raw side edge of the shirt. Repeat for the other end of the elastic. Zigzag stitch the elastic in place, over the raw edge of the turned up bottom edge of the shirt neck, holding the ends of the elastic firmly and stretching the elastic as you sew.

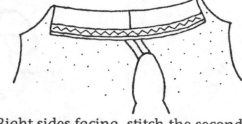

3. Right sides facing, stitch the second shirt shoulder seam.

4. Press 1" at the bottom edge of each sleeve to the wrong side. Cut two pieces of elastic 4" long each. Apply as you did for the neck.

5. Gather stitch the top edge of the sleeve. Match the dots on the sleeves to the dots on the shirt. Pin. Pull up on the gather threads. Adjust gathers. Pin. Stitch. Repeat for the second sleeve.

6. Stitch the sleeve/side seams.

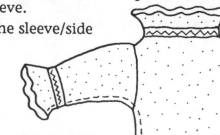

7. Press under ¼" at hem edge of shirt. Repeat. Topstitch.

Overalls

1. Right sides together, stitch inside leg seams on both pants pieces.

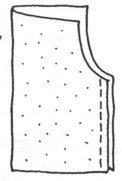

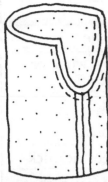

2. Turn one pants piece right side out. Put it inside the other pants piece, which is still wrong side out (right sides are thus facing). Match the long curved crotch seam. Stitch.

3. Press under ¼" at waist. Press under ½".

4. Press under ¼" at bottom edges of pants legs. Press under an additional 1". Topstitch over the turned under ¼".

5. Stitch three sides of the two bib pieces together, right sides facing. Turn right side out. Press. Turn under ¼" at bottom, unstitched edge of bib to inside, wrong side of bib. Press.

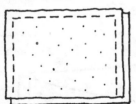 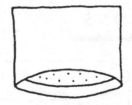

6. Pin bib to pants matching center crotch seam to the center of the bottom of the bib. Have the bottom edge of the bib inside the pants and even with the bottom folded edge of the turned under pants top.

7. Topstitch a scant ¼" from the folded, top edge of pants, sewing through all layers of pants and bib at front. Topstitch close to top folded edge of pants.

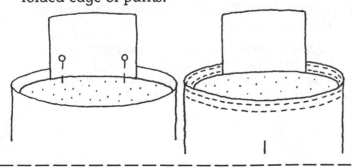

8. Press straps in half lengthwise. Press long edges to meet in center. Turn raw edges to inside on one end of straps. Topstitch close to folded edge.

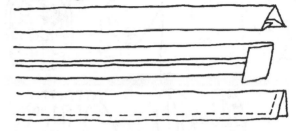

9. Decorative stitch along the pants hems, waist, three edges of the bib, and the straps. I used green, red, and yellow. Or stitch rickrack in place.

Pin and stitch unfinished ends of straps to inside back of pants 1¼" to either side of the center seam.

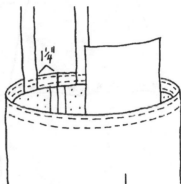

Bring straps over shoulders, pin them over top corners of bib to fit. Sew a button over them, through the bib.

Hair

1. Cut 200 8"-long pieces of yarn.

2. Draw a 3"-long line on a piece of paper. Put the top of the line under the presser foot. Stitch the centers of the lengths of the hair to the paper, filling the 3" evenly. Backstitch at the beginning and ends of the stitching.

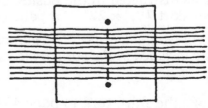

Tear away the paper.

3. Place the wig on the doll's head, with the seam as a part in the hair. Hand stitch in place. Trim the ends of the hair where needed. To keep the hair from falling in the doll's face, apply a little thinned glue to the top sides of the face. Press the hair to the glue and let dry.

Gretel

MATERIALS

1 skein yarn (I used Cotton Candy shade 2933, gingersnap by Brunswick)
¼ yard white cotton or print fabric for shirt
Matching thread
1 yard ¼"-wide elastic
¼ yard doe suede, corduroy, wool, or cotton for jumper
Matching thread
Two ½" silver buttons
Colored embroidery thread or rickrack
⅓ yard white cotton fabric for petticoat and drawers
1⅛ yards 1½"-wide gathered eyelet for petticoat and drawers
Two ¼" or ⅜" black shank buttons for shoes
One small basket

INSTRUCTIONS

Turn to page 16 for body instructions. When you have made the doll, painted or embroidered the face, and painted on the shoes, return here and continue to dress the doll and add the hair.

Prepare the patterns and cut and mark the fabric as instructed in the Basics. Cut the jumper skirt 7½" x 22". Cut petticoat 7" x 22".

Note: All seam allowances for clothing are ¼" and are included in the pattern pieces.

Shirt

To make the shirt, turn to page 48 in the instructions for Hansel.

Jumper

1. Right sides together, stitch the two short edges of the skirt together. This is the center back.

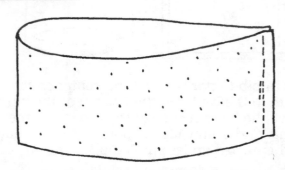

2. Press under ¼" at waist. Press under ½". This is the top edge of the skirt.

3. Press under ¼" along the remaining long edge of skirt. Repeat. Topstitch. This will be the hem edge.

4. Stitch three sides of the two bib pieces together, right sides facing. Turn right side out. Press. Turn under ¼" at bottom, unstitched edge of bib to inside. Press.

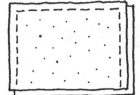

5. Find center front of skirt. Mark with a pin. Do the same for the bib.

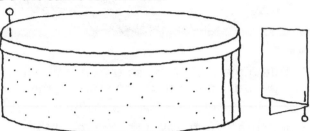

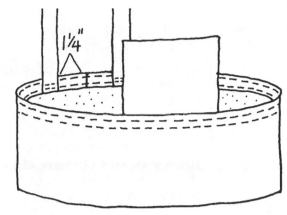

Pin bib to wrong side of skirt, matching pins. Have the bottom edge of the bib even with the bottom folded edge of the turned under skirt top.

6. Topstitch a scant ¼" from folded, top edge of skirt, sewing through all layers of skirt and bib at front. Topstitch again close to bottom folded edge.

Bring straps over shoulders, pin them over the top corners of the bib. Sew a button over them, through the bib.

Drawers

1. Fold one drawer piece in half the same way you cut it out, right sides facing. Stitch the inside leg seam. Repeat for the other drawer piece.

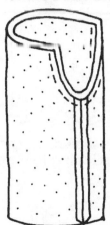

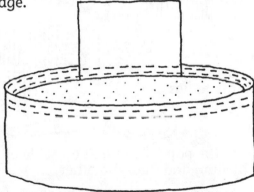

7. Press straps in half lengthwise. Press long edges to meet in center. Turn raw edges to inside on one end of straps. Topstitch close to folded edge.

2. Turn one drawer piece right side out. Put it inside the other drawer piece, which is still wrong side out (right sides are thus facing). Match the long, curved crotch seam. Stitch.

3. Turn drawers right side out. Press under ¼" on the top edge. Press under ½". Topstitch along the bottom fold, leaving a ½"-wide gap in the stitching for inserting elastic.

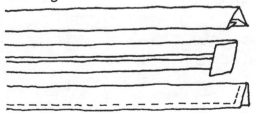

4. Cut a piece of elastic 9" long. Attach a safety pin to each end. Insert one safety pin into the casing. Work it all the way around and push it back out the opening. Overlap the ends of the elastic ½". Stitch them together.

8. Decorative stitch the skirt hem, skirt at waist, three edges of the bib, and the straps, or stitch rickrack. I used green, red, and yellow thread.

Pin and stitch unfinished ends of straps to inside back of skirt 1¼" to either side of the center seam.

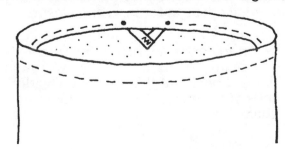

5. Press under ¹/₄" on the bottom edge of the drawer legs. Press under another ¹/₄".

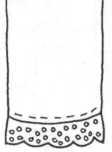

Cut two pieces of eyelet, each 8" long. Seam the two short edges of one piece together. Repeat for the second piece. Right side of eyelet facing wrong side of drawer leg, pin the top band of the eyelet to the turned under hem of the drawer leg. Stitch as shown.

Petticoat

1. Press under ¹/₄" on one long edge (making it the bottom edge) of the petticoat. Press under another ¹/₄".

Cut one piece of eyelet 22" long. Right side of eyelet facing wrong side of petticoat, pin the top band of the eyelet to the turned under hem of the petticoat. Stitch as shown.

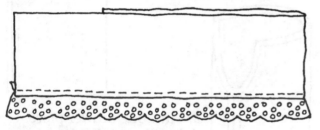

2. Fold the petticoat in half as shown. Stitch the short center back seam, including the eyelet.

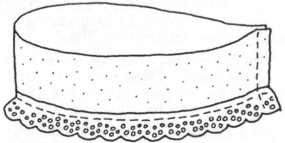

3. Press under ¹/₄" on the remaining long edge (the top edge). Press under ¹/₂". Topstitch along the bottom fold, leaving a ¹/₂"- wide opening for inserting elastic.

4. Cut a piece of elastic 9" long. Attach a safety pin to each end. Insert one safety pin into the casing. Work it all the way around and push it back out the opening. Overlap the ends of the elastic ¹/₂". Stitch them together.

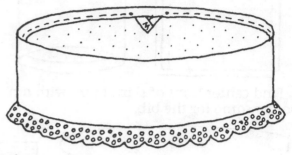

Hair

1. Fold a piece of paper so that it is 2" wide. Wrap yarn around it as shown until the wrapped yarn measures 2¹/₂" wide.

2. Machine stitch down the center of the yarn as shown, backstitching at the beginning and ends of the stitching.

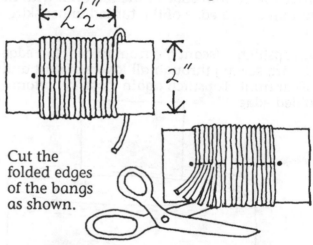

Cut the folded edges of the bangs as shown.

Tear the paper from first one side of the stitching and then the other.

3. Starting at one end of the skein, loop the remainder of the skein of yarn into an oval 28" wide as shown.

Tie a piece of yarn around one end of the oval as shown.

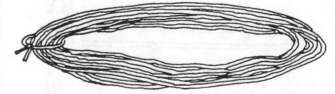

4. Draw a 3¹/₂"-long line on a piece of paper. Put it under the presser foot of your sewing machine. Lay the yarn on the paper as shown, having the tie you just made 2 ³/₄" to the left of the presser foot.

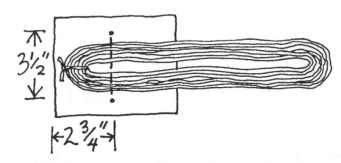

3½"

← 2 ¾" →

5. Stitch the yarn to the paper along the marked line, fitting all the hair in the 3½" space.

Tear one side of the paper and then the other from the stitching.

6. Hand stitch the machine stitching to the doll's head as if it were the part in the doll's hair.

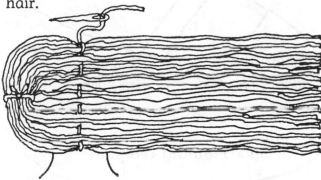

7. Smooth the yarn to the left of the part, the side you tied a piece of yarn around in step 3, and stitch to the left side of the head (looking at the doll's head from behind).

8. Tie a short piece of yarn or thread around the long length of yarn 2 ¾" to the right of the part. Hand stitch this point to the head.

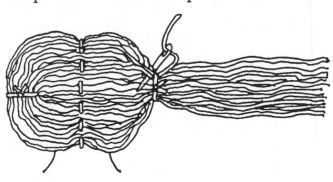

9. Clip the loops at the end of these long pieces of yarn. Braid the yarn. Bring the braid over the top of the head to the left side of the head (still looking from behind the doll). Decide where the braid will end, as the braid will now be too long and need to be

trimmed. About ¾" below this point, tie a piece of yarn or thread around the braid tightly. Trim the yarn extending beyond this point bluntly.

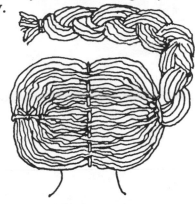

Tuck the end of the braid up under the braid and stitch the braid end in place.

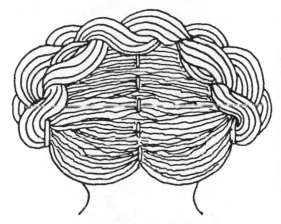

Continue stitching the braid over the head.

10. Stitch the bangs to the head as shown.

11. Tie bows as shown in the photograph.

Basket

Cut a piece of fabric and stuff into basket. Hand stitch the basket handle to the doll's hand.

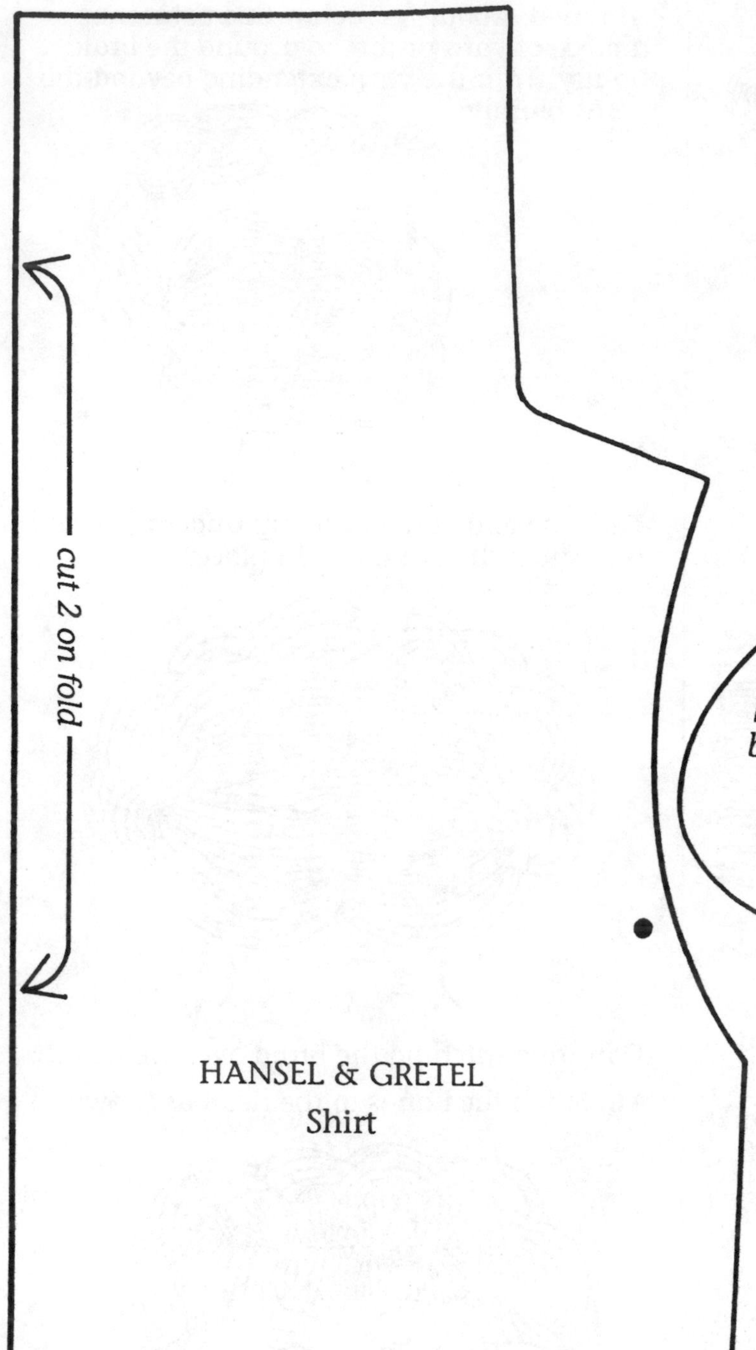

cut 2 on fold

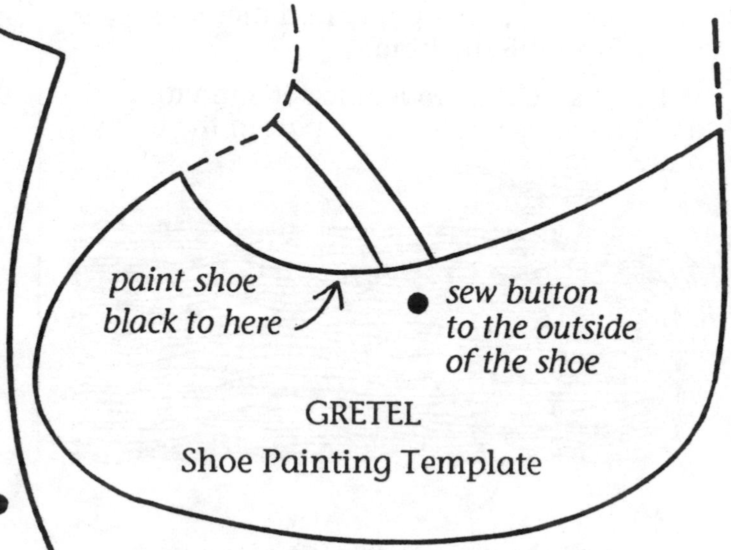

paint shoe black to here ↗

sew button to the outside of the shoe

GRETEL
Shoe Painting Template

HANSEL & GRETEL
Shirt

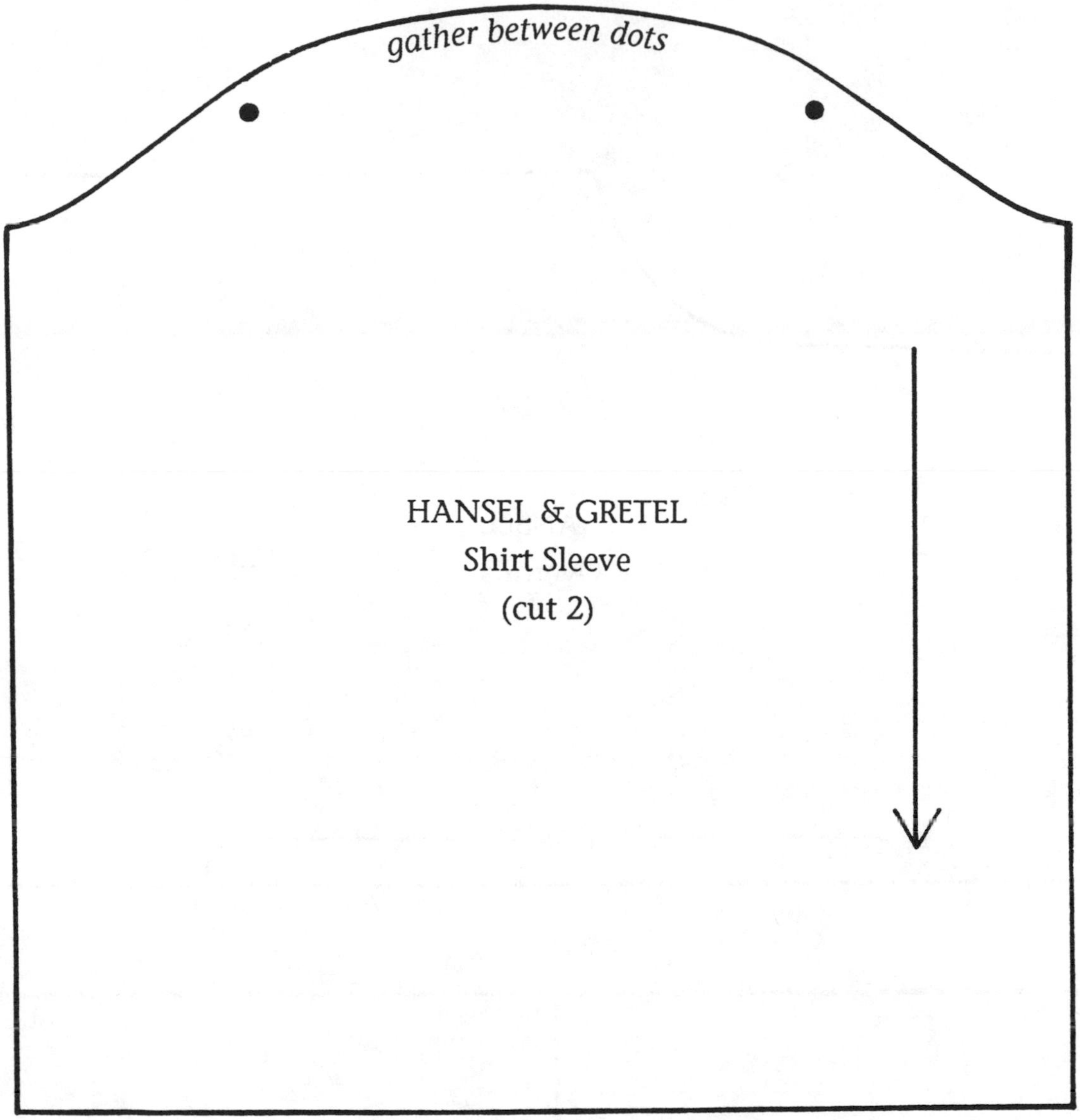

gather between dots

HANSEL & GRETEL
Shirt Sleeve
(cut 2)

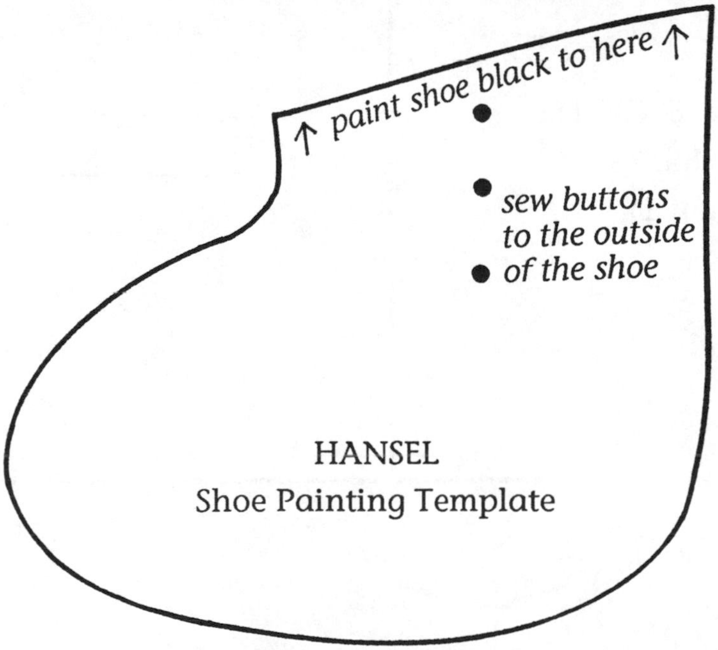

↑ *paint shoe black to here* ↑

*sew buttons
to the outside
of the shoe*

HANSEL
Shoe Painting Template

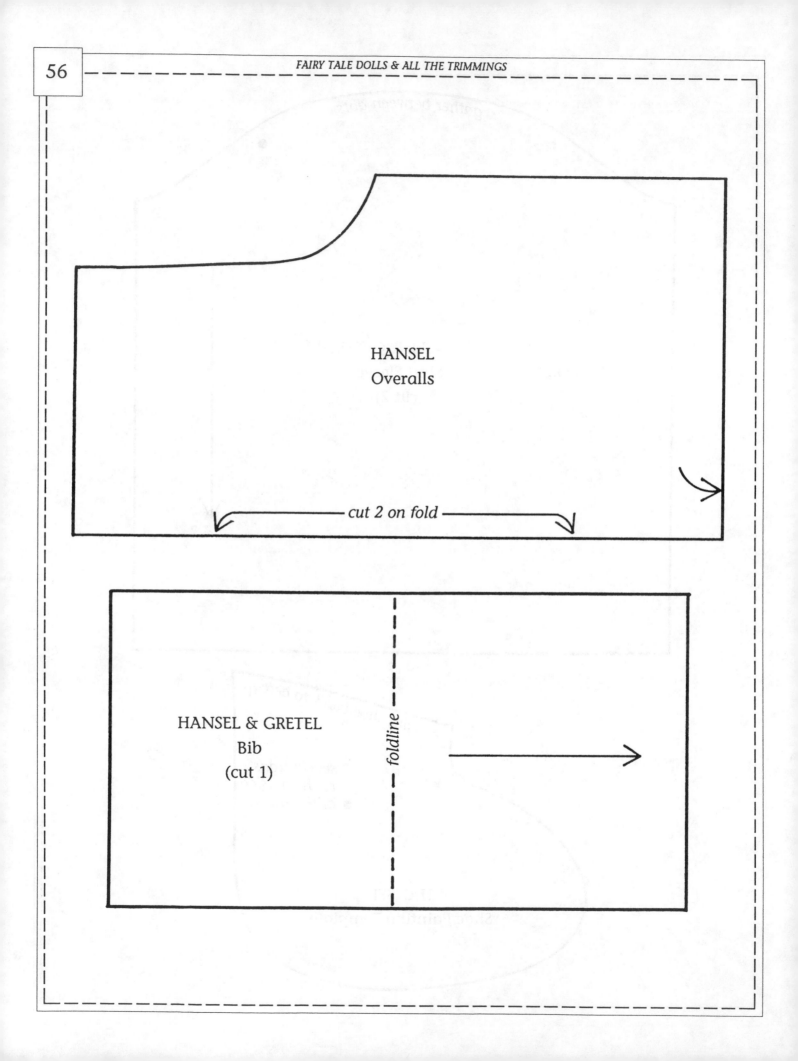

HANSEL
Overalls

cut 2 on fold

HANSEL & GRETEL
Bib
(cut 1)

foldline

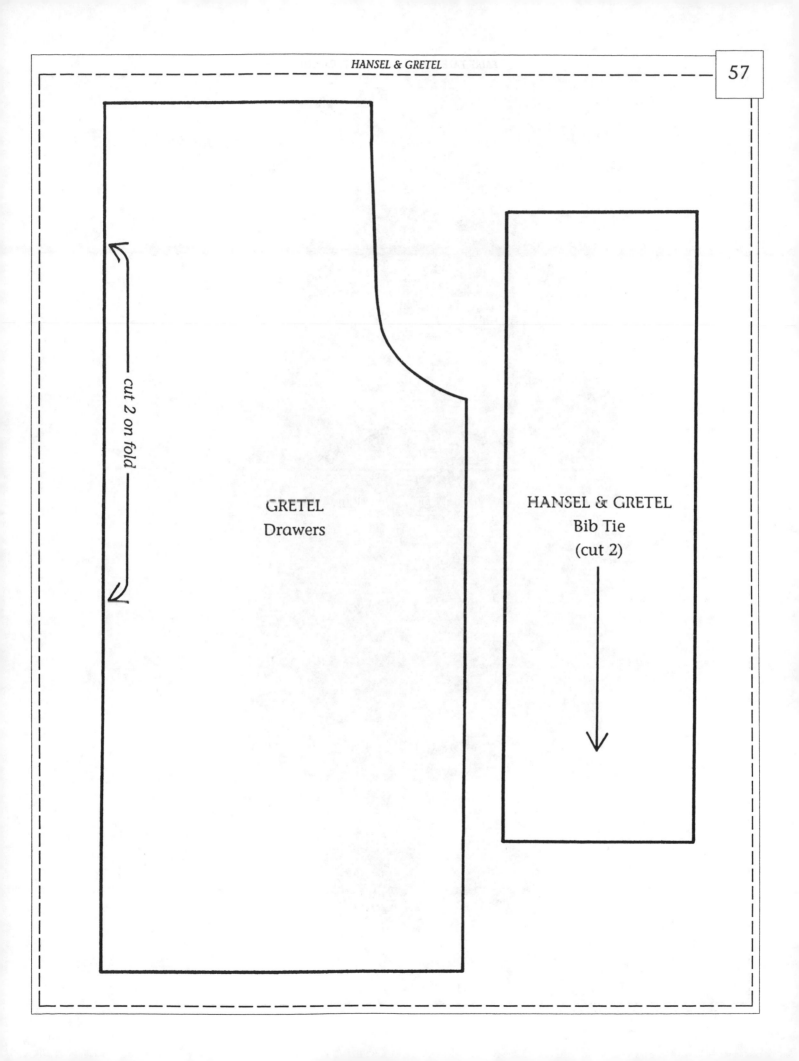

cut 2 on fold

GRETEL
Drawers

HANSEL & GRETEL
Bib Tie
(cut 2)

Goldilocks

Any child (or grown-up) will gladly share a meal and a warm bed with this little sweetheart.

Turn to page 116 to stitch up a family of bears to keep Goldilocks company.

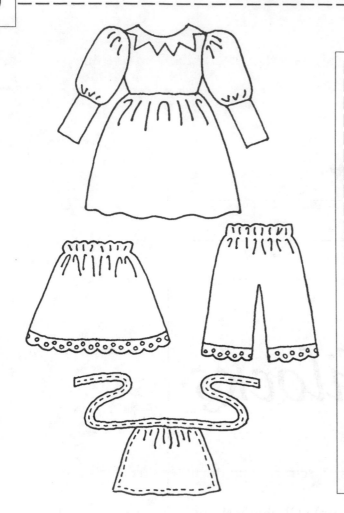

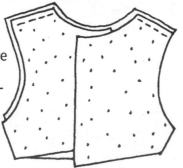

MATERIALS

1 skein yarn (I used Cotton Candy shade 2903 by Brunswick)
⅓ yard dress fabric
⅓ yard 2"-wide gathered lace or eyelet for dress collar
Matching thread
Two ¼" buttons for dress
¼ yard apron fabric
Matching thread
1 yard ⅜"-wide ribbon for hair bows and front dress bow
⅓ yard white or natural cotton fabric for petticoat and drawers
1⅛ yards 1½"-wide gathered eyelet for petticoat and drawers
½ yard ¼"-wide elastic
Two ¼" or ⅜" black or brown shank buttons for shoes

INSTRUCTIONS

Turn to page 16 for body instructions. When you have made the doll, painted or embroidered the face, and painted on the shoes, return here and continue to dress the doll and add the hair.

Prepare the patterns and cut and mark the fabric as instructed in the Basics. Cut dress skirt 6¼" x 22". Cut petticoat 7" x 22". Cut apron 5½" x 7". Cut one apron tie 1½" x 24".

Note: All seam allowances for clothing are ¼" and are included in the pattern pieces.

Dress

1. Right sides facing, stitch two front bodice pieces to one back bodice piece at shoulders. Repeat for second set; one will be the bodice, one the lining.

Cut the lace for the collar 9" long. To finish the short raw edges, press one short cut edge ¼" to the wrong side. Repeat. Topstitch. Repeat for the other short cut end of the lace collar. Pin the lace collar to the neck edge of one bodice front/backs, right sides facing. Baste.

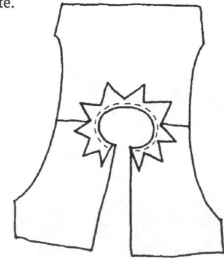

2. Right sides facing, pin bodice to bodice lining along neck edge and center backs, matching shoulder seams. Stitch. Clip curves. Trim corners. Turn.

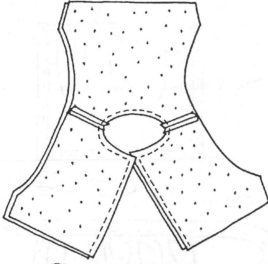

3. Using a long machine stitch, gather the top and bottom edges of the sleeve top between the dots. Matching the dots on sleeve top and sleeve bottom, pin the bottom straight edge of the sleeve top to the sleeve bottom, right sides facing. Pull up on gather stitches to fit. Pin. Adjust gather stitches. Pin. Stitch.

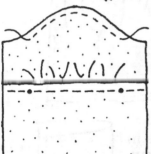

From now on, treat the two layers as one. Press 1/4" on the bottom edge of the sleeves to the wrong side. Repeat. Topstitch.

4. Match and pin dots on sleeve top to dots on bodice, treating bodice and bodice lining as one. Pull up on gather stitches. Even out the fullness between the dots and pin. Stitch through sleeve, bodice, and bodice lining. Repeat for other sleeve.

5. Right sides together, sew the underarm and side seams as one.

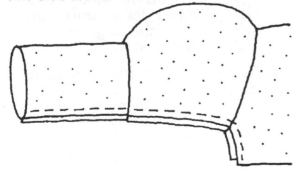

6. Match and pin the two short sides of the dress skirt, right sides facing. Using a 1/2" seam allowance, stitch center back seam of dress skirt. Start with a basting stitch, sew half way down the center back seam of the dress skirt. Change to a regular sewing stitch. Backstitch a few stitches. Sew to the bottom edge of the skirt. Backstitch.

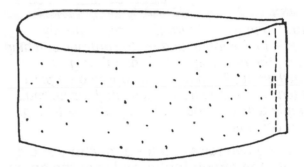

Press the seam open. Turn under 1/4" on each seam allowance. For the hem, press under 1/4" on the skirt bottom (remember that the basting stitches are at the top end of the skirt) and then another 1/4". Starting at the one side of the top of the center back seam, continuing around the hem of the skirt and up the other side of the center back seam of the skirt, topstitch. Remove basting stitches.

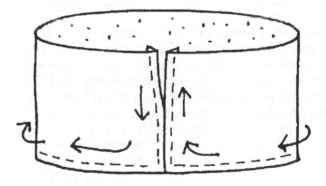

7. Using two rows of gathering stitches, gather the top edge of the skirt starting 1 1/2" from the center back opening edges. Pin the skirt to the bottom edge of the bodice (through both layers), right sides facing, matching center backs. Adjust gathers. Pin. Stitch.

8. Make buttonholes on bodice as marked. Try on doll. Mark positions for buttons. Sew buttons on.

Apron

1. On two short apron edges, press raw edge 1/4" to wrong side. Repeat. Do the same for one long edge. Topstitch.

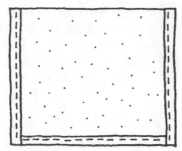

Tip: Often when I turn the corner with my needle in the fabric and try to continue stitching along the next edge I find the fabric gets bunched up. Try placing the apron on a piece of tear-away stabilizer. Then stitch as normal. Simply tear the stabilizer away after stitching. So much easier!

2. Using two rows of a long machine stitch, gather the remaining raw edge of the apron.

3. Press the apron tie in half lengthwise. Open the fold up again and turn the long raw edges in to meet at the fold in the center. Press. Turn the short raw edges in 1/4".

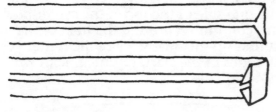

4. Unfold the tie. Find the center of the tie. Place a pin 1" to one side of this point. (This will make the tie lengths uneven. When you tie the apron on the doll you won't find that one tie is much longer than the other.) Measure 1 7/8" to each side of the first pin. Mark with pins. Remove the first pin. Right sides facing, pin the raw edge of the apron to one raw edge of the tie, matching the apron side edges to the pins on the apron tie. Pull up on the gathering stitches and gather the apron to fit the tie. Distribute the gathers evenly. Pin. Stitch.

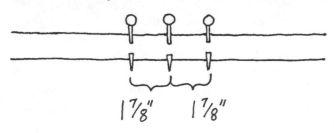

Fold the tie over the raw edges of the apron as pressed. Pin. Topstitch starting at the far end of one tie.

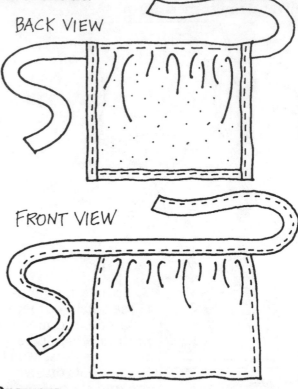

BACK VIEW

FRONT VIEW

Drawers

1. Fold one drawer piece in half the same way you cut it out, right sides facing. Stitch the inside leg seam. Repeat for the other drawer piece.

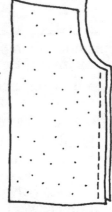

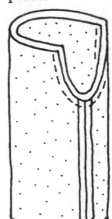

2. Turn one drawer piece right side out. Put it inside the other drawer piece, which is still wrong side out (right sides are thus facing). Match the long, curved crotch seam. Stitch.

3. Turn drawers right side out. Press under 1/4" on the top edge. Press under 1/2". Topstitch along the bottom fold, leaving a 1/2"-wide gap in the stitching for inserting elastic.

4. Cut a piece of elastic 9" long. Attach a safety pin to each end. Insert one safety pin into the casing. Work it all the way around and push it back out the opening. Overlap the ends of the elastic 1/2". Stitch them together.

5. Press under 1/4" on the bottom edge of the drawers legs. Press under another 1/4".

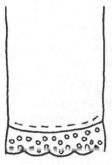

Cut two pieces of eyelet, each 8" long. Seam the two short edges of one piece together. Repeat for the second piece. Right side of eyelet facing wrong side of drawer leg, pin the top band of the eyelet to the turned under hem of the drawer leg. Stitch as shown.

Petticoat

1. Press under 1/4" on one long edge (making it the bottom edge) of the petticoat. Press under another 1/4".

Cut one piece of eyelet 22" long. Right side of eyelet facing wrong side of petticoat, pin the top band of the eyelet to the turned under hem of the petticoat. Stitch as shown.

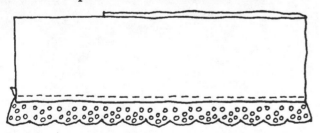

2. Fold the petticoat in half as shown. Stitch the short center back seam, including the eyelet.

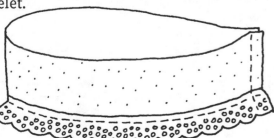

3. Press under 1/4" on the remaining long edge (the top edge). Press under 1/2". Top-stitch along the bottom fold, leaving a 1/2" or so wide opening for inserting elastic.

4. Cut a piece of elastic 9" long. Attach a safety pin to each end. Insert one safety pin into the casing. Work it all the way around and push it back out the opening. Overlap the ends of the elastic 1/2". Stitch them together.

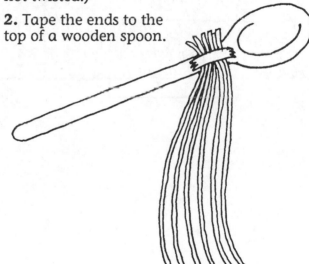

Hair

1. Undo the skein of yarn and divide it into six pieces of roughly equal length. Put them together so they are one length of six strands. (Just like embroidery floss, though not twisted.)

2. Tape the ends to the top of a wooden spoon.

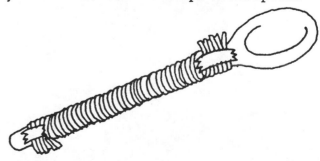

3. Wrap the yarn around the spoon. Clip the yarn at the bottom and tape to the spoon.

4. Dilute the stiffener by one half with water. Use a paint brush to saturate the yarn on the spoon. Set aside on a paper towel to drip. Put on the rack of the oven. Leave in the oven at 200°F until it is dry, turning once. This will take 10-20 minutes. Set aside to cool. Remove the yarn from the spoon.

Continue this curling process until you have used all of the yarn.

Lay the curled yarn on a table so it is relaxed, fully curled. Measure each curl in turn. Trim them so they are about 10" long. There is no need to be precise. Measure the pieces you trimmed from the 10"-long pieces. Reserve any that measure 6" or longer.

Draw a line on a piece of paper 5" long. Place the paper so the top of the line is under the presser foot of your sewing machine. Find the center of one 10"-long curl of yarn. Lay it centered on the paper at the top of the drawn line. Stitch the yarn to the paper.

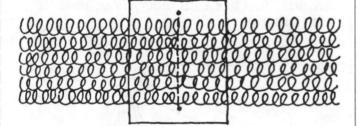

Add yarn, one curl at a time, stitch it, add another curl, stitch it, and so on until you've used all of the 10" curls. Now add the remaining shorter pieces. If you've used up all of the 5" line, start over again at the top of the line, putting these curls on top of the curls you already stitched to the paper. The end of the paper with the shorter curls can go at the back of the head.

Clip the threads from your stitching. Tear one side of the paper from the stitching and then the other.

Fold the wig in half so it will be double thick.

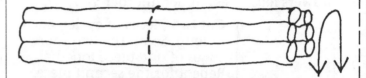

Starting at the doll's forehead, place the wig on the doll. Stitch the seam to the head. Arrange the curls. Trim any ends as necessary.

Make three bows from the hair ribbon. Pull the few front-most curls on one side of the face up and to the side. Stitch the bows over and through the curls to hold them in place. Repeat for the other side.

Stitch a bow to the front of the doll's dress as in photograph.

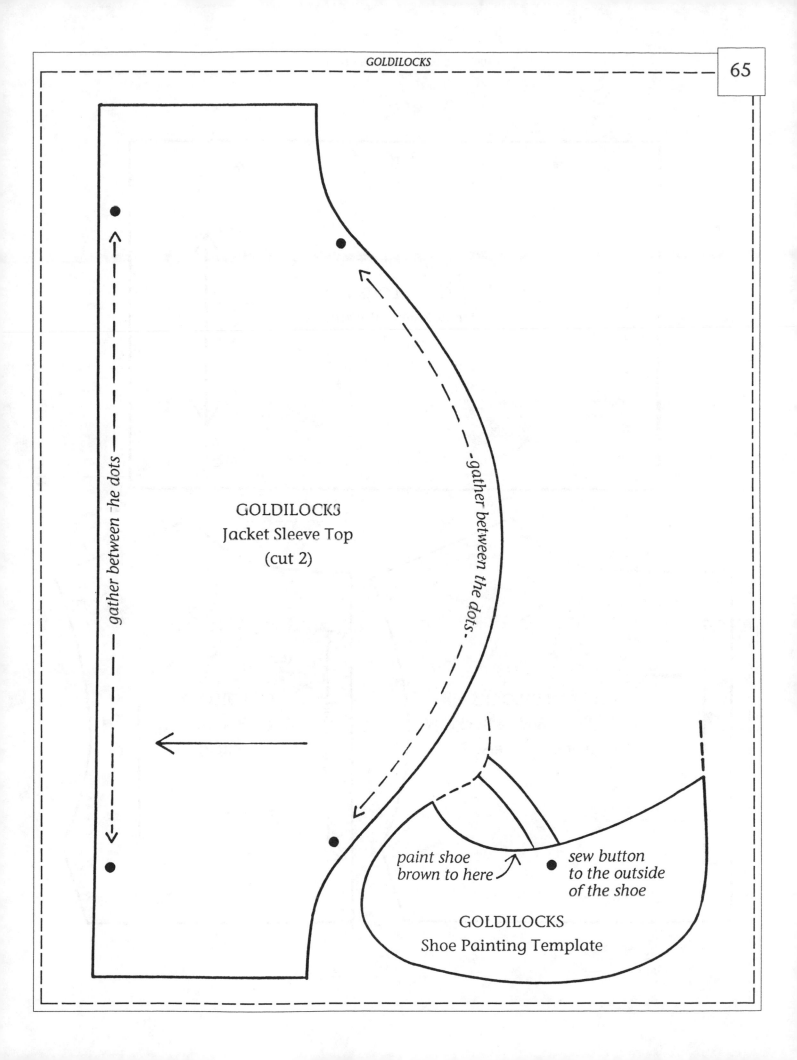

gather between the dots

gather between the dots

GOLDILOCKS
Jacket Sleeve Top
(cut 2)

paint shoe
brown to here

sew button
to the outside
of the shoe

GOLDILOCKS
Shoe Painting Template

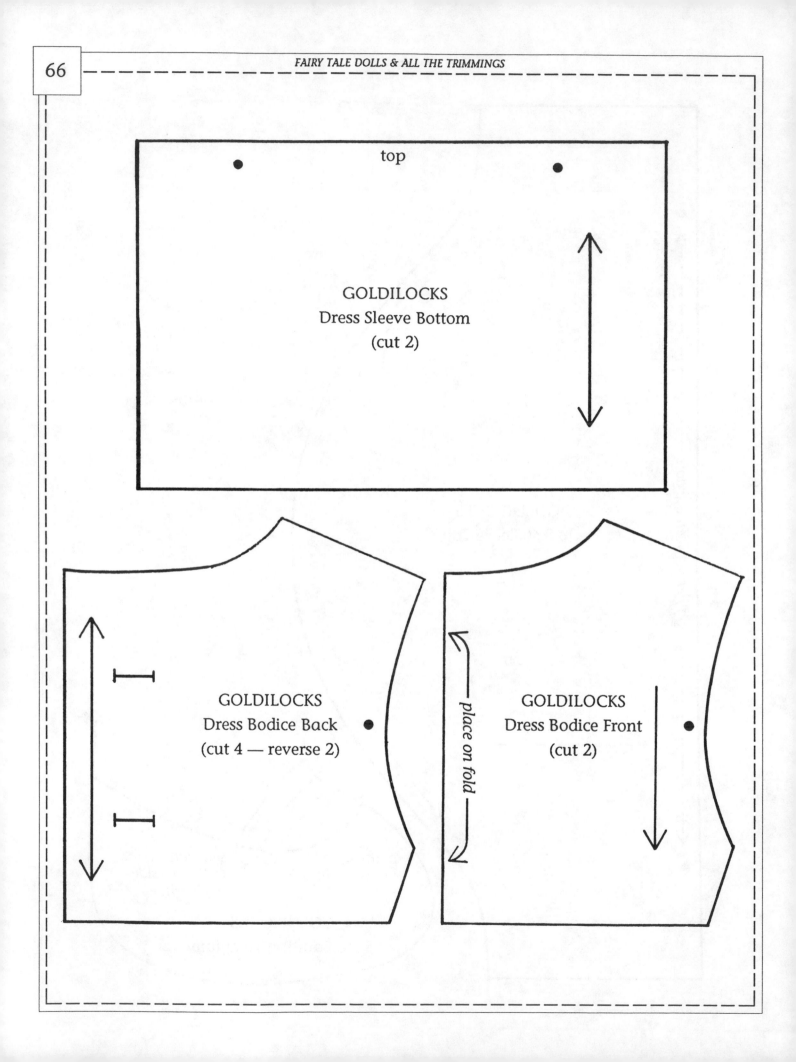

top

GOLDILOCKS
Dress Sleeve Bottom
(cut 2)

GOLDILOCKS
Dress Bodice Back
(cut 4 — reverse 2)

place on fold

GOLDILOCKS
Dress Bodice Front
(cut 2)

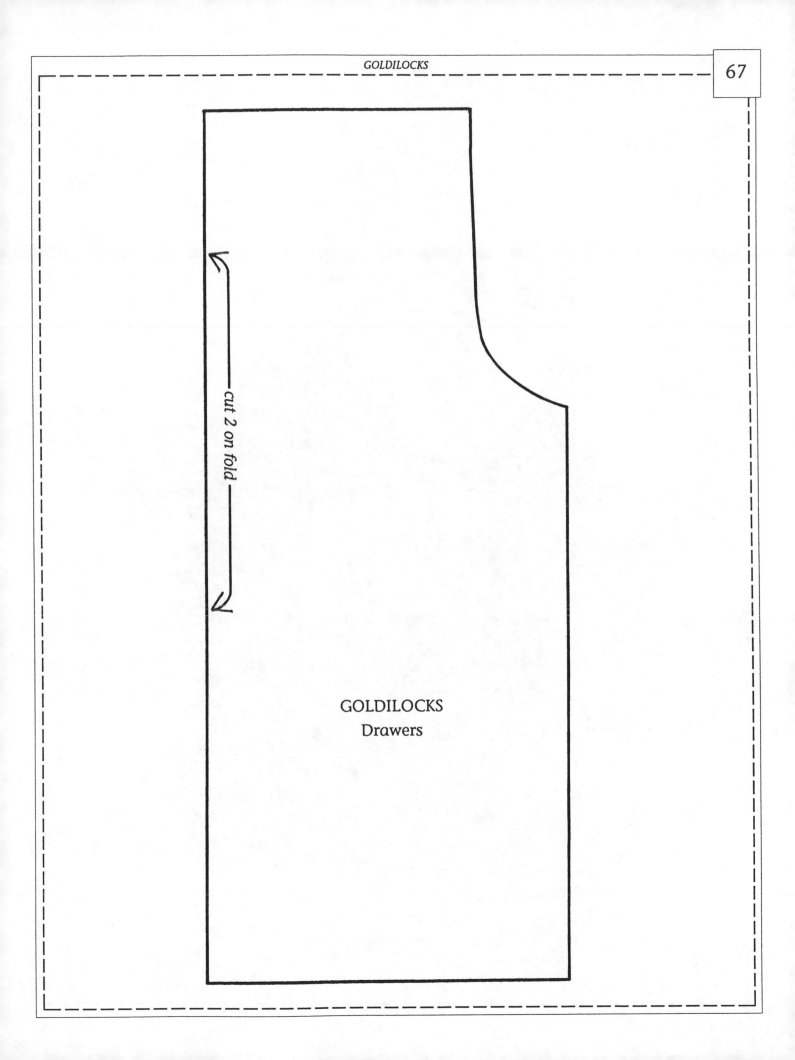

cut 2 on fold

GOLDILOCKS
Drawers

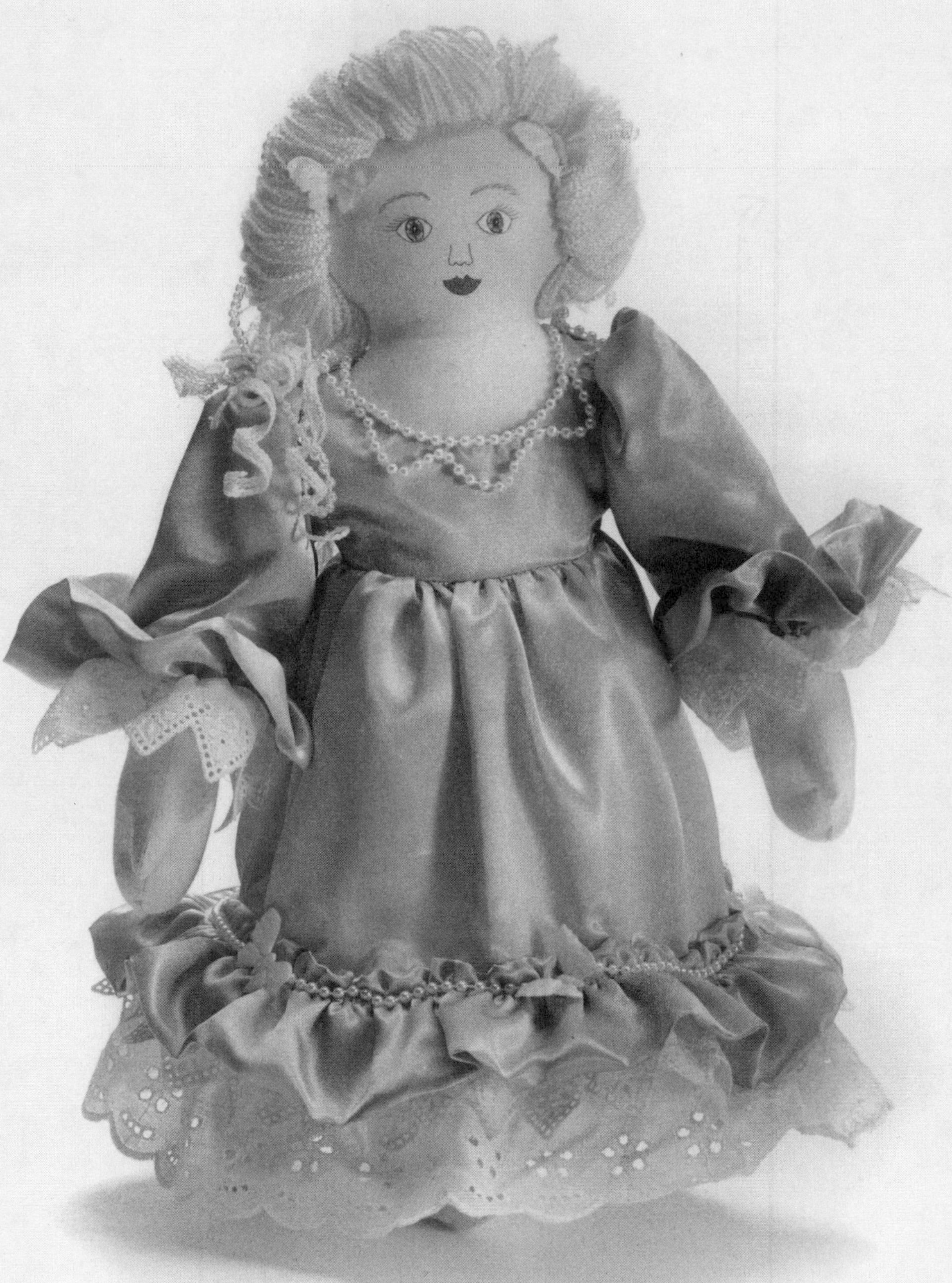

♥

Cinderella

Thanks to her Fairy Godmother, Cinderella is ready for the ball. From her bejeweled hair to her glass slippers, she is truly a princess.

♥

MATERIALS

¹/₂ yard silk-like fabric for dress

Matching thread

⁷/₈ yard 2¹/₂"-wide lace for hem and cuffs

⁵/₈ yard 3¹/₂"-wide lace for hem

2 yards ¹/₈"-wide pearls-by-the-yard

2 skeins yarn
(I used Silky Baby 082307 by Sirdar)

Stiffy™

Butterflies or jewels to decorate
hem and hair

¹/₈ yard clear plastic (find it in the
decorator section of the fabric store)

¹/₂ yard fine netting for petticoat

⁵/₈ yard ¹/₄"-wide elastic

INSTRUCTIONS

Turn to page 16 for body instructions. When you have made the doll, and painted or embroidered the face, return here and continue to dress the doll and add the hair and shoes.

Prepare the patterns and cut and mark the fabric as instructed in the Basics. Cut a rectangle for the dress skirt 7¹/₂" x 22". Cut a 6" x 36" rectangle for the skirt ruffle. Cut two 4" x 18" rectangles for the sleeve ruffles. Using the full width of the netting for the petticoat. Trim the cut edges evenly so that the petticoat measures the width of the netting and is 16" tall.

Note: All seam allowances for clothing are ¹/₄" and are included in the pattern pieces.

Dress

1. Right sides facing, stitch two front bodice pieces to one back bodice piece at shoulders. Repeat for second set; one set will be the bodice, one the lining.

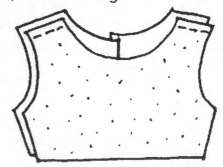

2. Pin bodice to bodice lining along neck edge and center backs, matching shoulder seams. Stitch. Clip curves. Trim corners. Turn. Press.

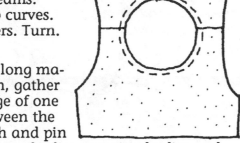

3. Using a long machine stitch, gather the top edge of one sleeve between the dots. Match and pin dots to dots on bodice, treating bodice and bodice lining as one. Pull up on gather stitches. Even out the fullness between the dots and pin. Stitch through sleeve, bodice, and bodice lining. Repeat for other sleeve.

4. Right sides together, sew the under arm and side seams as one.

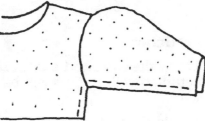

5. Stitch the two short edges of one sleeve ruffle together, right sides facing. Fold in half along the length of the rectangle. Baste the raw edges together. Gather the raw edges. Pull up on the gather threads. Pin to the bottom of the sleeve. Adjust to match the sleeve. Stitch.

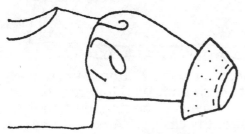

Cut a piece of the narrower lace 8" long. Seam the short edges together. With the right side of the lace against the underside of the sleeve ruffle, stitch the lace to the seam allowances of the ruffle/sleeve.

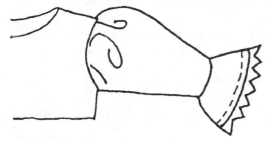

Cut a piece of elastic 5" long. Overlap the ends ¼ and stitch them together. Stretch to fit the seam allowances of the sleeve ruffle/ sleeve. Zigzag.

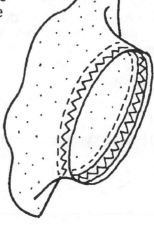

Repeat for the second sleeve.

6. Using a ½" seam allowance, stitch the center back seam of the dress skirt. Start with a basting stitch, sew half way down, and change to a regular sewing stitch. Backstitch a few stitches. Sew to the bottom edge of the skirt. Backstitch.

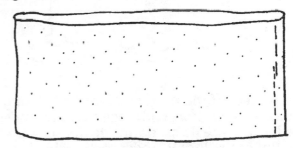

Press the seam open. Press under ¼" on each seam allowance. Repeat. For the hem, press under ¼" on the skirt bottom (remember that the basting stitches are at the top end of the skirt) and then another ¼". Topstitch, starting at one side of the top of the center back seam, continuing around the hem of the skirt and up the other side of the center back seam of the skirt. Remove the basting stitches.

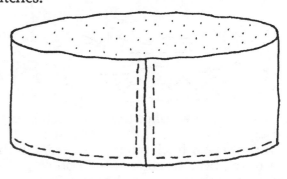

7. Stitch the two short edges of the skirt ruffle together, right sides facing. Wrong sides facing, match and baste the long raw edges of the ruffle together. Fold so that the seam is at the back. Gather stitch 1/2" from one folded edge.

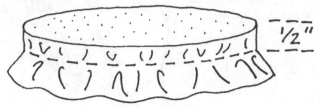

Pull up on the gather threads. Adjust to fit the bottom edge of the dress. Pin the gather stitching over the hem. Stitch the ruffle to the hem.

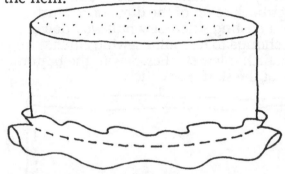

Cut a piece of the narrower lace 22 1/2" long. Seam the two short ends together. Pin under the hem of the dress, right side up, so that the top of the lace is under the machine stitching securing the ruffle to the hem. Baste.

Repeat for the wider lace. Stitch.

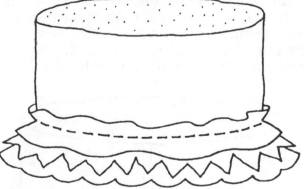

8. Using two rows of gathering stitches, gather the top edge of the skirt starting 1 1/2" from the center back opening edges. Pin the skirt to the bottom edge of the bodice (through both layers), right sides facing, matching center backs. Adjust gathers. Pin. Stitch.

9. Make buttonholes on bodice as marked. Try on doll. Mark positions for buttons. Sew buttons on.

10. Hand stitch beads over the stitching on the skirt ruffle. Hand stitch beads to the bodice as shown.

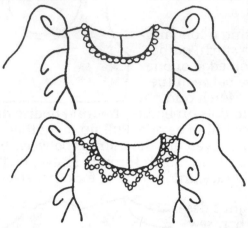

Petticoat

1. Sew the two short edges (16" long) of the netting together. This will be the center back seam.

2. Fold the netting so that the seam overlaps. Stitch 1/2" from the fold, leaving a 1/2" gap in the stitching.

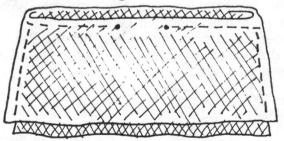

3. Cut a piece of elastic 9" long. Attach a safety pin to each end. Working from between the two layers of netting, push one safety pin into the casing. Work it all the way around. Emerge out of the gap again. Overlap the ends of the elastic 1/4". Stitch. Put the petticoat on the doll.

Hair

1. For the curls, wrap yarn around the handle of a wooden spoon, four strands at a time. Secure the ends with tape. Thin Stiffy™ with an equal amount of water. Using a paint brush, saturate the yarn with the Stiffy™ solution. Put in a 200°F oven for 15 minutes or until dry. Set aside to cool. Remove from spoons. Trim tape off ends of yarn. With four wooden spoons, I did three batches of hair for one doll.

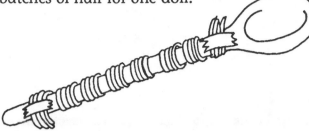

2. Draw a 6" line on a piece of paper. Repeat on another piece of paper. Put one piece of paper under your sewing machine so that the top of the line is under the presser foot.

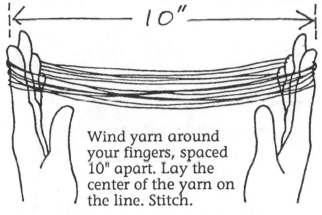

Wind yarn around your fingers, spaced 10" apart. Lay the center of the yarn on the line. Stitch.

Repeat until you have filled the two lines with yarn. Pull the paper from the stitching. Stitch the machine stitching to the doll's head as shown.

FRONT

BACK

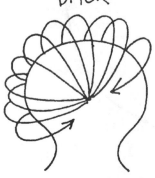

3. Pull all of the folds in the yarn to the back of the head. Run a needle through the folds to stitch the yarn to the back of the doll's head.

LOOP THREAD AROUND YARN

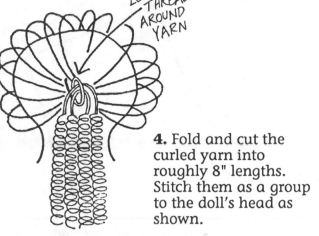

4. Fold and cut the curled yarn into roughly 8" lengths. Stitch them as a group to the doll's head as shown.

5. Tack beads to the doll's hair as shown.

Shoes

1. Stitch two shoe pieces together. Trim seam allowances. Turn right side out. Put on doll.

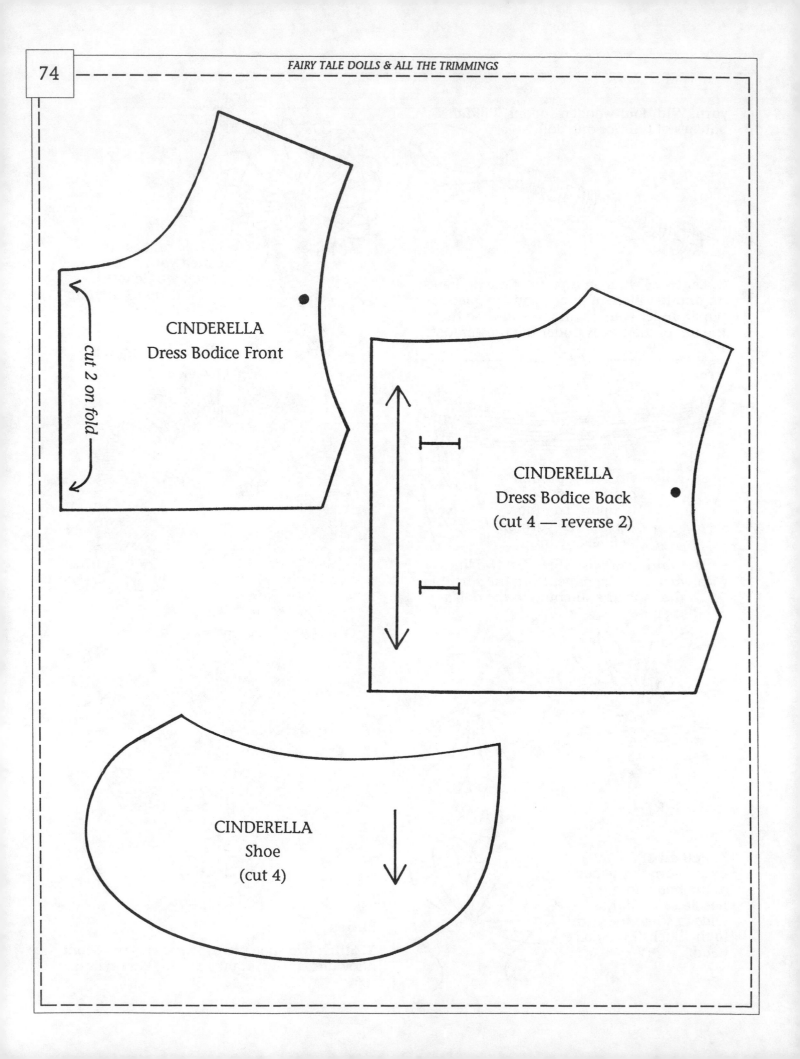

CINDERELLA
Dress Bodice Front

cut 2 on fold

CINDERELLA
Dress Bodice Back
(cut 4 — reverse 2)

CINDERELLA
Shoe
(cut 4)

gather between dots

CINDERELLA
Sleeve
(cut 2)

♥

Fairy Godmother

Grant all of Cinderella's wishes with this
heaven-sent lady. I used silky fabrics in
pastel colors of lavender and soft green
for my Fairy Godmother's dress. I added
peachy eyelet wings and silver shoes. Her
hair is soft blue-pink yarn mixed with a
shiny silver and gray yarn.

She's sure to charm people of all ages.

♥

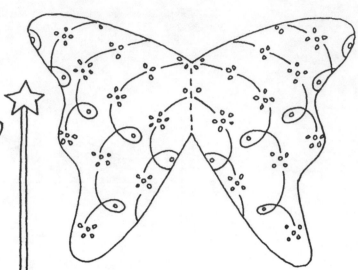

INSTRUCTIONS

Turn to page 16 for body instructions. When you have made the doll, and painted or embroidered the face, return here and continue to dress the doll and add her hair and shoes.

Prepare the patterns and cut and mark the fabric as instructed in the Basics. Cut a rectangle for the dress skirt 9" x 22". Cut two 4" x 18" rectangles for the top sleeve ruffle. Cut two 6" x 18" rectangles for the lower sleeve ruffles. Use the full width of the netting for the petticoat. Trim the cut edges evenly so that the petticoat rectangle measures the width of the netting (selvedge to selvedge) and 16" tall.

Note: All seam allowances for clothing are ¼" and are included in the pattern pieces.

MATERIALS

½ yard silk-like fabric for bodice, sleeves, top sleeve ruffle, and overskirt

Matching thread

⅓ yard silk-like fabric to coordinate for lower sleeve ruffle and underskirt

Matching thread

¾ yard pearls-by-the-yard

Stars and jewels to decorate hair and underskirt

⅛ yard stretchy fabric for shoes (I used a metallic color)

½ yard fine netting for petticoat

⅝ yard ¼"-wide elastic

⅜ yard fabric for wings (I used peach eyelet)

Matching thread

⅜ yard medium to heavyweight fusible interfacing

One skein each Hayfield Reflections color 6002 and Unger Aura color 2862

7"-long ¼" dowel

Gold paint

Gold glitter paint

Star for the wand (Crystal jewel)

Dress

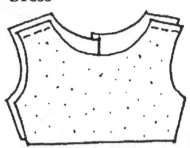

1. Right sides facing, stitch two front bodice pieces to one back bodice piece at shoulders. Repeat for second set; one set will be the bodice, one the lining.

2. Pin bodice to bodice lining along neck edge and center backs, matching shoulder seams. Stitch. Clip curves. Trim corners. Turn. Press.

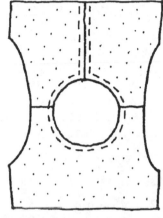

3. Using a long machine stitch, gather the top edge of one sleeve between the dots. Match and pin dots to dots on bodice, treating bodice and bodice lining as one. Pull up on gather stitches. Even out the fullness between the dots and pin. Stitch through sleeve, bodice, and bodice lining. Repeat for other sleeve.

4. Right sides together, sew the underarm and side seams as one.

5. Stitch the two short edges of one top sleeve ruffle together, right sides facing. Fold in half along the length of the rectangle. Baste the raw edges together. Repeat for the lower sleeve ruffle. Put the top sleeve ruffle inside the lower sleeve ruffle.

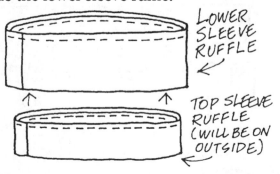

LOWER SLEEVE RUFFLE

TOP SLEEVE RUFFLE (WILL BE ON OUTSIDE)

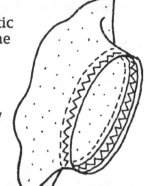

Match the raw edges. Gather the raw edges. Pull up on the gather threads. Pin to the bottom of the sleeve so that the top, narrower ruffle is against the sleeve. Adjust to match the sleeve. Stitch.

Cut a piece of elastic 5" long. Overlap the ends 1/4" and stitch them together. Stretch to fit the seam allowances of the sleeve ruffle/sleeve. Zigzag.

Repeat for the second sleeve.

6. Using a 1/2" seam allowance, stitch the center back seam of dress skirt. Start with a basting stitch, sew half way down and change to a regular sewing stitch. Backstitch a few stitches. Sew to the bottom edge of the skirt. Backstitch.

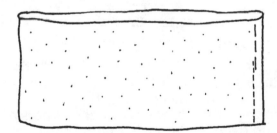

Press the seam open. Press under 1/4" on each seam allowance. Repeat. For the hem, press under 1/4" on the skirt bottom (remember that the basting stitches are at the top end of the skirt) and then another 1/4". Topstitch, starting at one side of the top of the center back seam, continuing around the hem of the skirt and up the other side of the center back seam of the skirt. Remove the basting stitches.

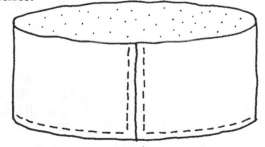

7. Using two rows of gathering stitches, gather the top edge of the skirt starting 1 1/2" from the center back opening edges. Pin the skirt to the bottom edge of the bodice (through both layers), right sides facing, matching center backs. Adjust gathers. Pin. Stitch.

8. Make buttonholes on bodice as marked. Try on doll. Mark positions for buttons. Sew buttons on.

Overskirt

1. Gather stitch the long, curved edge of the overskirt top piece.

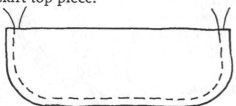

2. Right sides facing, pin the overskirt top to the overskirt base, pulling up on the gather threads to fit. Stitch.

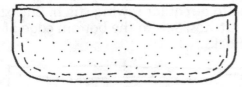

3. Turn right side out. Match the raw edges at the top of the overskirt together. Baste.

4. Cut a piece of elastic 8" long. Overlap the ends 1/4". Stitch the ends together. Zigzag stitch the elastic to the seam allowances of the top overskirt base, stretching the elastic to fit.

5. Tack the elastic to the back of the underskirt in a few places so that it doesn't flip up and show the seam allowances. Put the overskirt on the doll over the dress.

Petticoat

1. Seam the two short edges (16" long) of the netting together. This will be the center back seam.

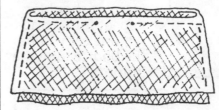

2. Fold the netting so that the seam overlaps. Stitch 1/2" from the fold, leaving a 1/2" gap in the stitching.

3. Cut a piece of elastic 9" long. Attach a safety pin to each end. Working from between the two layers of netting, push one safety pin into the casing. Work it all the way around. Emerge out of the gap again. Overlap the ends of the elastic 1/4". Stitch. Put the petticoat on the doll.

Wings

1. Cut the wing fabric into two pieces.

2. Following the manufacturer's instructions, apply the interfacing to the wrong side of one of the wing fabric pieces.

3. Wrong sides together, satin stitch the two wing fabrics together along the marked lines. Trim away the extra wing fabric along the outside of the satin stitching.

4. Tack the middle of the wings to the back of the doll's dress.

Hair

1. Draw a 6" line on a piece of paper. Repeat on another piece of paper. Put one piece of paper under your sewing machine so that the top of the line is under the presser foot.

2. Wind yarn around your fingers, spaced 10" apart. Use about twice the amount of the blue/green yarn as the silver/gray yarn. Lay the center of the yarn on the line. Stitch.

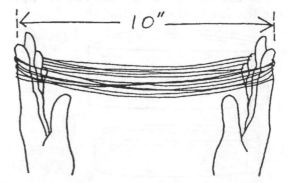

Repeat until you have filled the two lines with yarn. Pull the paper from the stitching. Stitch the machine stitching to the doll's head as shown.

3. Pull all of the folds in the yarn to the back of the head. Run a needle through the folds to stitch the yarn to the back of the doll's head.

4. Tack pearls to the doll's head as shown.

5. Glue jewels to the front of the dress skirt and to the doll's hair. Stitch pearls along the neckline of the dress bodice.

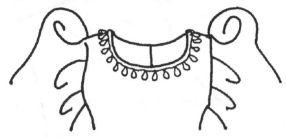

Shoes

1. Right sides facing, stitch two shoe pieces together. Repeat. Turn one set right side out. Put it inside the other set. Match and pin the top raw edges. Stitch.

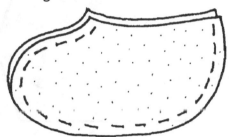

2. Slash one shoe. Turn right side out. Put the lining (slashed) shoe inside the shoe. Put on doll.

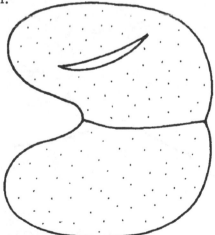

Wand

1. Paint the wand gold. When dry, paint with gold glitter paint. Set aside to dry.

2. Glue the star to the top of the wand. If it is not a double-sided star, glue two stars to the top of the wand, back-to-back.

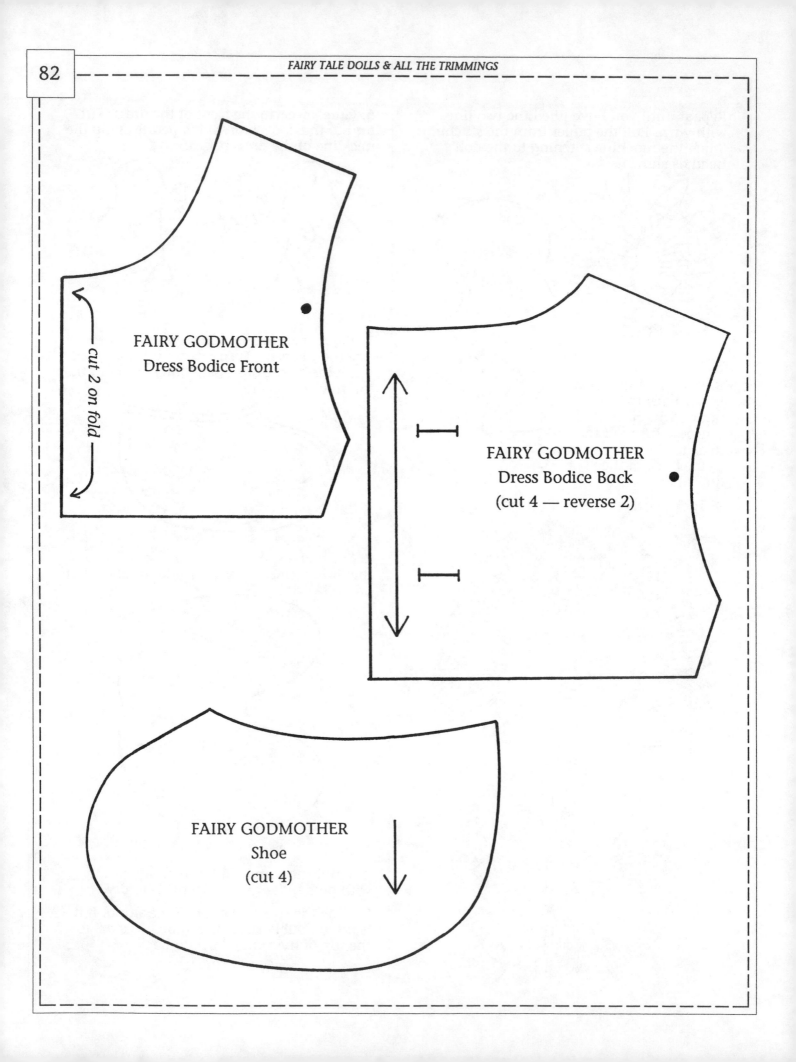

FAIRY GODMOTHER
Dress Bodice Front

cut 2 on fold

FAIRY GODMOTHER
Dress Bodice Back
(cut 4 — reverse 2)

FAIRY GODMOTHER
Shoe
(cut 4)

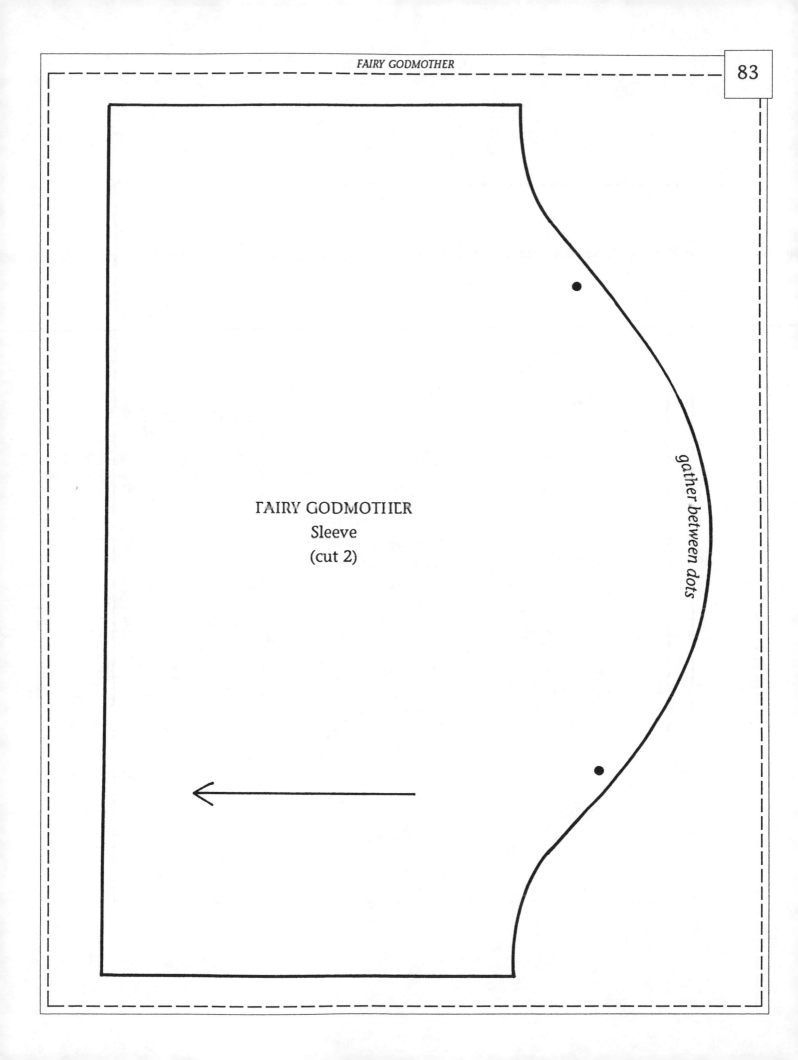

FAIRY GODMOTHER
Sleeve
(cut 2)

gather between dots

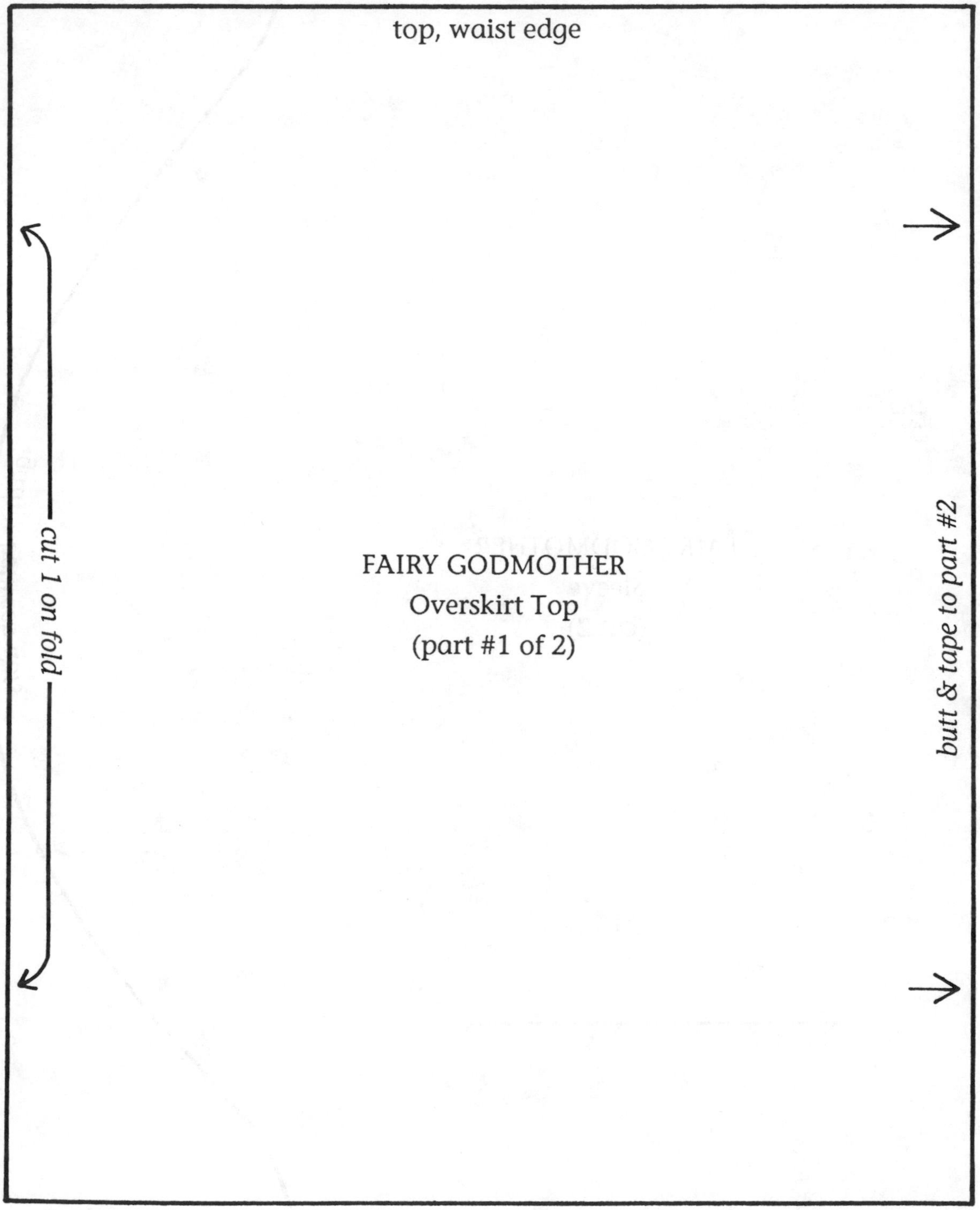

top, waist edge

cut 1 on fold

butt & tape to part #2

FAIRY GODMOTHER
Overskirt Top
(part #1 of 2)

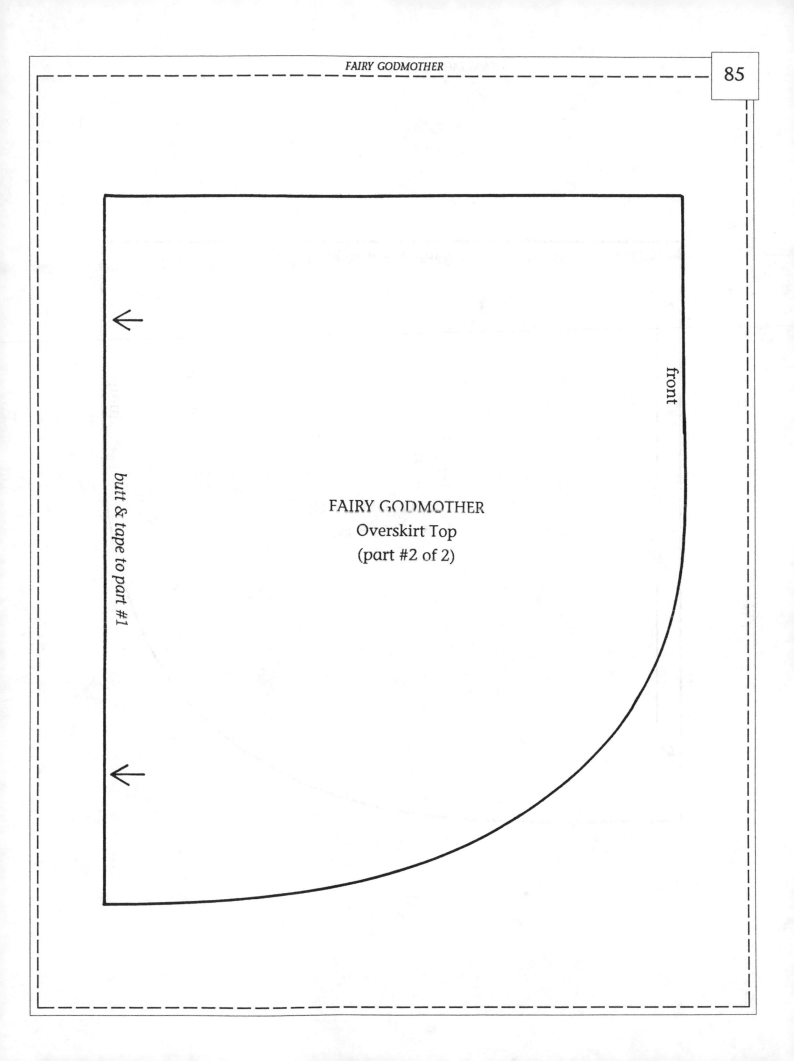

butt & tape to part #1

front

FAIRY GODMOTHER
Overskirt Top
(part #2 of 2)

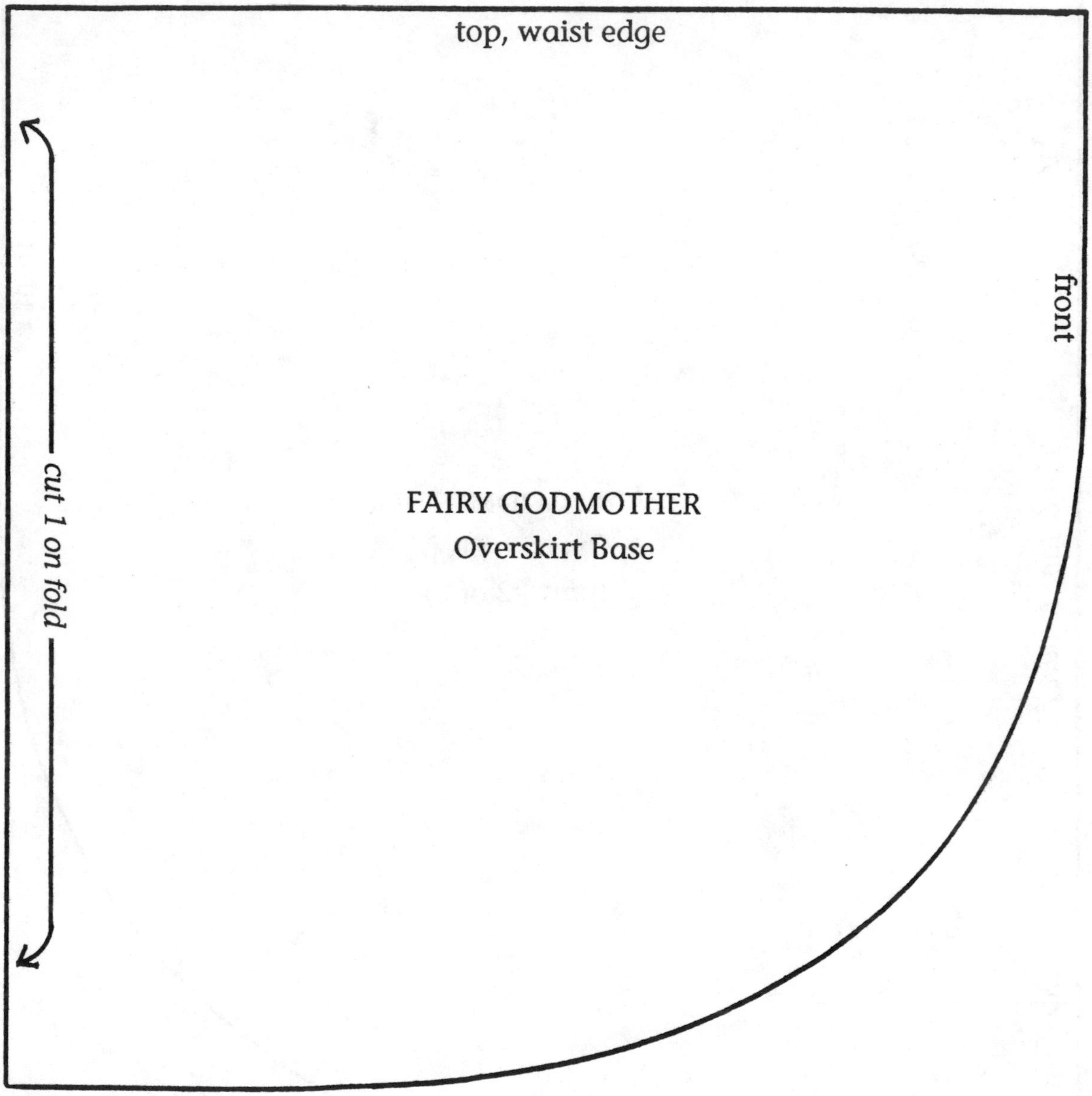

top, waist edge

front

cut 1 on fold

FAIRY GODMOTHER
Overskirt Base

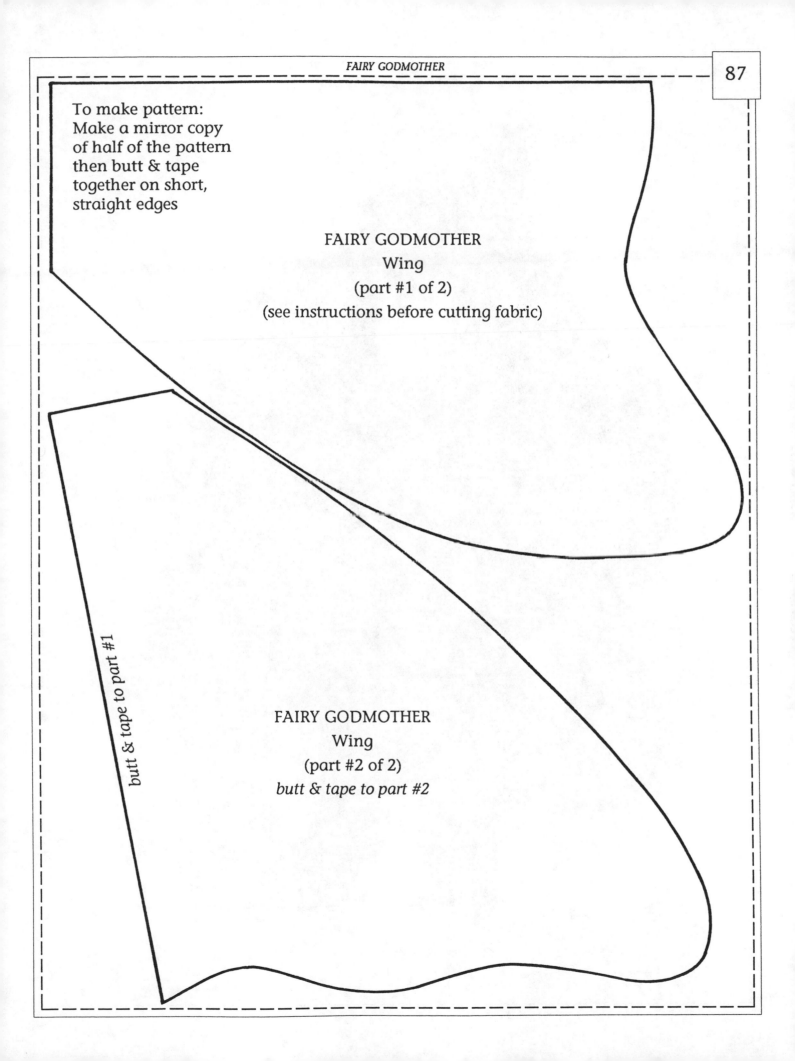

To make pattern:
Make a mirror copy
of half of the pattern
then butt & tape
together on short,
straight edges

FAIRY GODMOTHER
Wing
(part #1 of 2)
(see instructions before cutting fabric)

butt & tape to part #1

FAIRY GODMOTHER
Wing
(part #2 of 2)
butt & tape to part #2

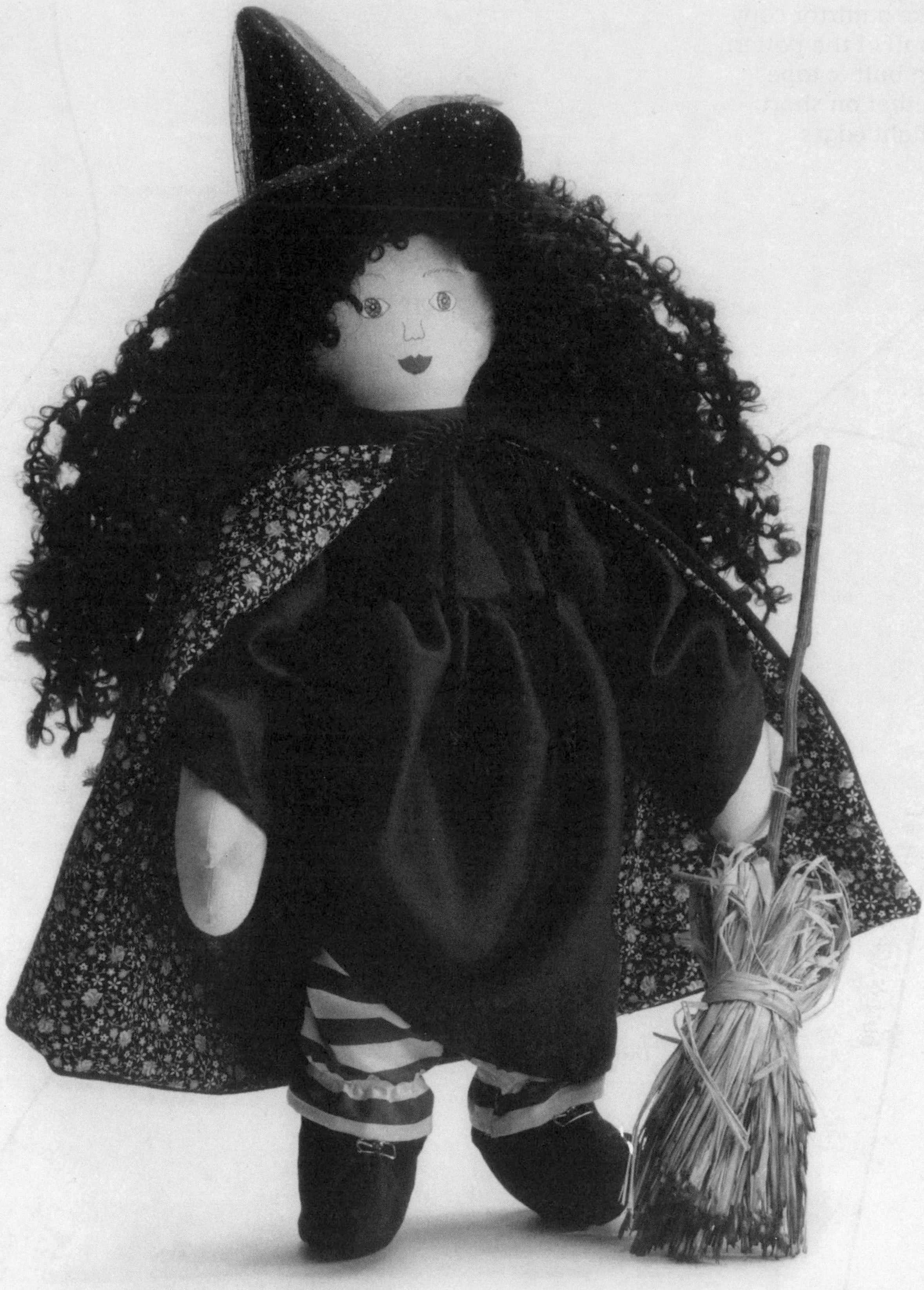

♥

Witch

Custom tailor this witch to suit your taste. Mine is dressed in traditional black garb, but has a sweet smile. Yours can be green and ugly. Add more adornments to suit your fancy: glitter, metallic stars on her dress, a spider hanging from her hat.

♥

MATERIALS

1 yard black fabric for dress and cape
(I used a rayon blend)

Matching thread

½ yard cape lining

⅝ yard ribbon or roping for cape ties

⅓ yard red-and-white striped fabric for
bloomers

Matching thread

½ yard ¼"-wide elastic

One 6"-wide felt hat (see Sources)

1 skein Sirdar Persian black and 1 skein
Phildar Clapotis green

½ yard black netting,
with gold glitter, if possible

¼ yard stretch material for shoes
(I used a stretch velvet)

Two gold buckles for shoes
(see Sources)

Raffia

12" stick or dowel

INSTRUCTIONS

Turn to page 16 for body instructions.
When you have made the doll, and painted
or embroidered the face, return here and
continue to dress the doll and add her hair
and shoes.

Prepare the patterns and cut and mark the
fabric as instructed in the Basics. Cut dress
skirt 9" x 22".

*Note: All seam allowances for clothing are ¼"
and are included in the pattern pieces.*

Dress

1. Right sides facing, stitch two front bodice
pieces to one back bodice piece at shoulders.
Repeat for second set; one will be the bodice,
one the lining.

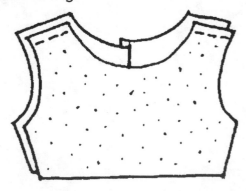

2. Pin bodice to bodice lining along neck edge and center backs, matching shoulder seams. Stitch. Clip curves. Trim corners. Turn right side out. Press.

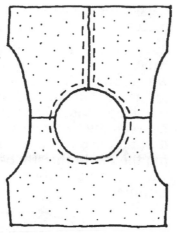

3. Using a long machine stitch, gather the top edge of one sleeve between the dots. Match and pin dots to dots on bodice, treating bodice and bodice lining as one. Pull up on gather stitches. Even out the fullness between the dots and pin. Stitch through sleeve, bodice, and bodice lining. Repeat for other sleeve.

4. Right sides together, sew the underarm and side seams as one.

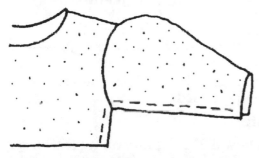

5. Press ¹/₄" on the bottom edge of the sleeves to the wrong side. Repeat. Topstitch.

6. Match and pin the two short sides of the dress skirt, right sides facing. Using a ¹/₂" seam allowance, stitch center back seam of dress skirt. Starting with a basting stitch, sew half way down the center back seam of the dress skirt. Change to a regular sewing stitch. Backstitch a few stitches. Sew to the bottom edge of the skirt. Backstitch.

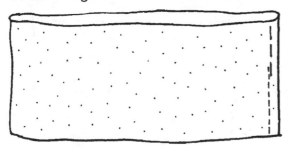

Press the seam open. Turn under ¹/₄" on each seam allowance. For the hem, press under ¹/₄" on the skirt bottom (remember that the basting stitches are at the top end of the skirt) and then another ¹/₄". Topstitch, starting at the one side of the top of the center back seam, continuing around the hem of the skirt and up the other side of the center back seam of the skirt. Remove basting stitches.

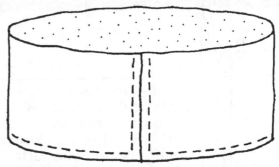

7. Using two rows of gathering stitches, gather the top edge of the skirt starting 1¹/₂" from the center back opening edges. Pin the skirt to the bottom edge of the bodice (through both layers), right sides facing, matching center backs. Adjust gathers. Pin. Stitch.

8. Make buttonholes on bodice as marked. Try on doll. Mark positions for buttons. Sew buttons on.

Drawers

1. Press under ¹/₄" on the bottom edge of each drawer leg. Press under another ¹/₄". Topstitch.

2. Cut a piece of elastic 4" long. Pin it to the wrong side of the bottom of one drawer leg, 1¹/₂" above the bottom edge of the leg. Stretch to fit. Zigzag in place.

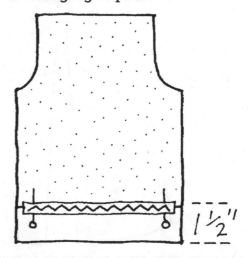

1¹/₂"

3. Right sides together, fold one drawer piece in half the same way you cut it out, right sides facing. Stitch the inside leg seam. Repeat for the other drawer piece.

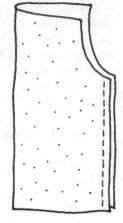

4. Turn one drawer piece right side out. Put it inside the other drawer piece, which is still wrong side out (right sides are thus facing). Match the long, curved crotch seam. Stitch.

5. Turn drawers right side out. Press under ¹/₄" on the top edge. Press under ¹/₂". Topstitch along the bottom fold, leaving a ¹/₂"-wide gap in the stitching for inserting elastic.

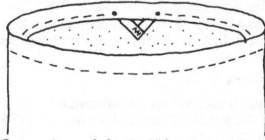

6. Cut a piece of elastic 9" long. Attach a safety pin to each end. Insert one safety pin into the casing. Work it all the way around and push it back out the opening. Overlap the ends of the elastic ¹/₂". Stitch them together.

Cape

1. Right sides facing, stitch the two cape front pieces to the cape back piece as shown.

Repeat for the cape lining front and back pieces.

2. Right sides facing, pin the cape to the cape lining, matching the raw edges all the way around. Put the ties inside, between the layers, so that the ends of the ties stick out of the openings. (Dotted lines show ties in between the two layers.) Stitch all the way around the outside edges of the cape, catching the ties in the stitches and leaving a 3"-wide opening at the center bottom back for turning.

Turn right side out. Press. Slip stitch the opening closed.

Hair

3. Draw a 3"-long line on a piece of paper. Loop the black yarn into a 20"-long pile until you have used up about one quarter of the skein. Move the pile to the sewing machine and stitch the center of the yarn to the line on the paper. Repeat three more times, using up the entire skein. Add small batches of 20"-long green yarn throughout the black hair. Use about ¹/₄ of the skein of the green yard in total. If you run out of room on the line, stitch more yarn on top of the yarn already stitched.

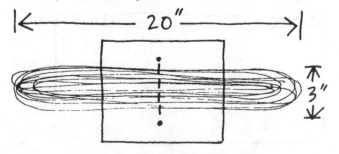

2. Stitch the machine stitching "part" to the center of the doll's head as shown, starting 1¾" below the seam at the top of the doll's head and continuing down the back of the head. The stitching in the yarn will form a "part" in the doll's hair.

Hat

1. Place the center of the netting over the top of the hat. Arrange the fullness of the netting into folds around the crown of the hat. Tack the netting to the hat as shown.

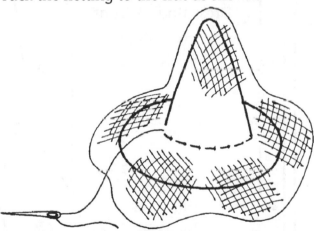

2. Tuck the ends of the netting inside the crown of the hat. Trim away extra netting if it won't fit inside the crown.

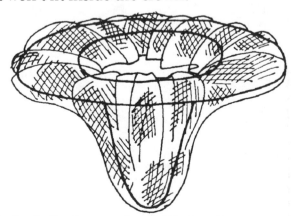

3. Tack the hat to the doll's head.

Shoes

1. Right sides facing, stitch two shoe pieces together as shown.

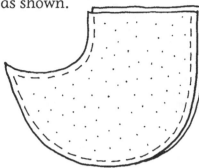

2. Press the top edges of the shoe down ¼". Topstitch.

Repeat steps 1 and 2 for the second shoe. Turn shoes right side out. Tack a buckle to the front of each shoe. Stuff the toes of the shoes with fiberfill. Put on doll.

Broom

1. Have your glue gun warmed up. Cut a stick or dowel 10" to 12" long. Fold a fistful of raffia in half. Put hot glue on one end of the stick. Insert into the raffia.

2. Tie a long piece of raffia or string around the broom as shown.

Trim the ends of the raffia.

3. If desired, singe the ends of the broom in the flame of a hurricane lamp or your evening fire. Keep a bucket of water close at hand to immerse the broom in to stop the burning.

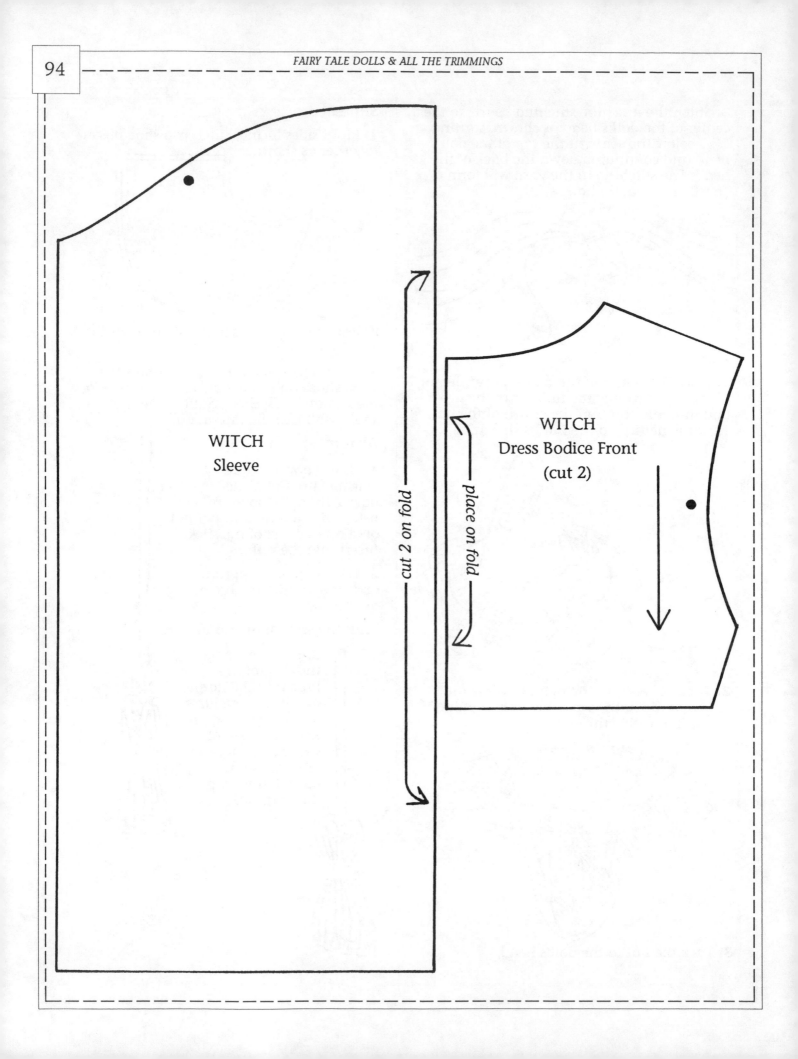

WITCH
Sleeve

cut 2 on fold

WITCH
Dress Bodice Front
(cut 2)

place on fold

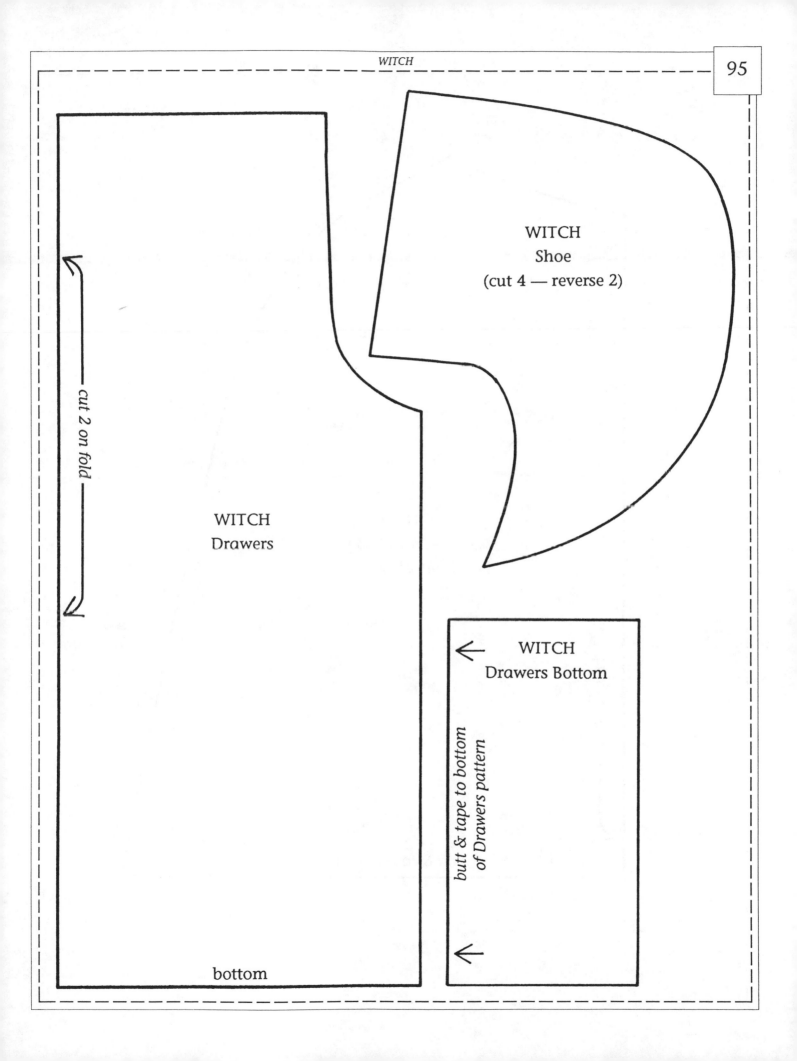

WITCH
Shoe
(cut 4 — reverse 2)

cut 2 on fold

WITCH
Drawers

WITCH
Drawers Bottom

*butt & tape to bottom
of Drawers pattern*

bottom

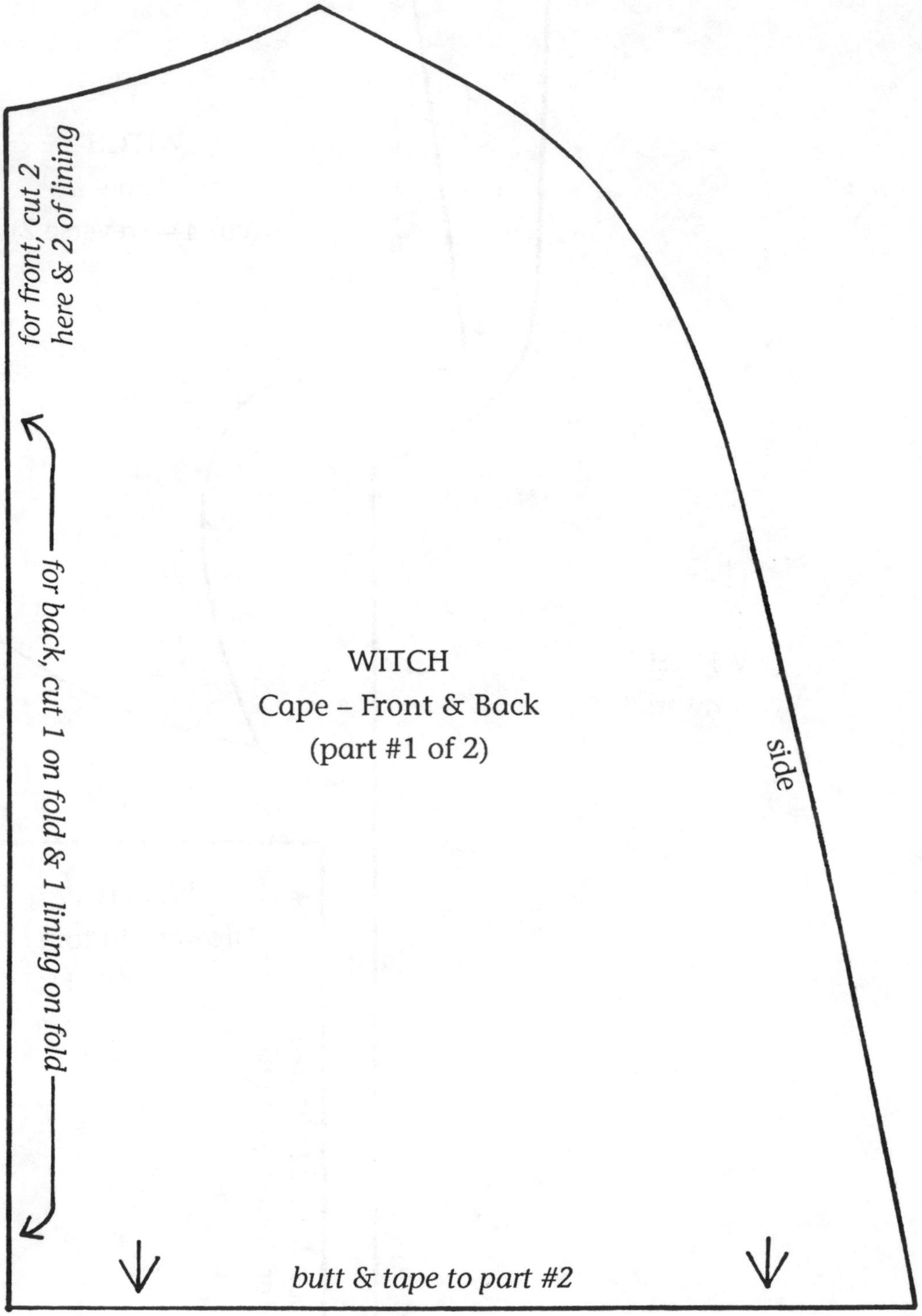

for front, cut 2 here & 2 of lining

for back, cut 1 on fold & 1 lining on fold

WITCH
Cape – Front & Back
(part #1 of 2)

side

butt & tape to part #2

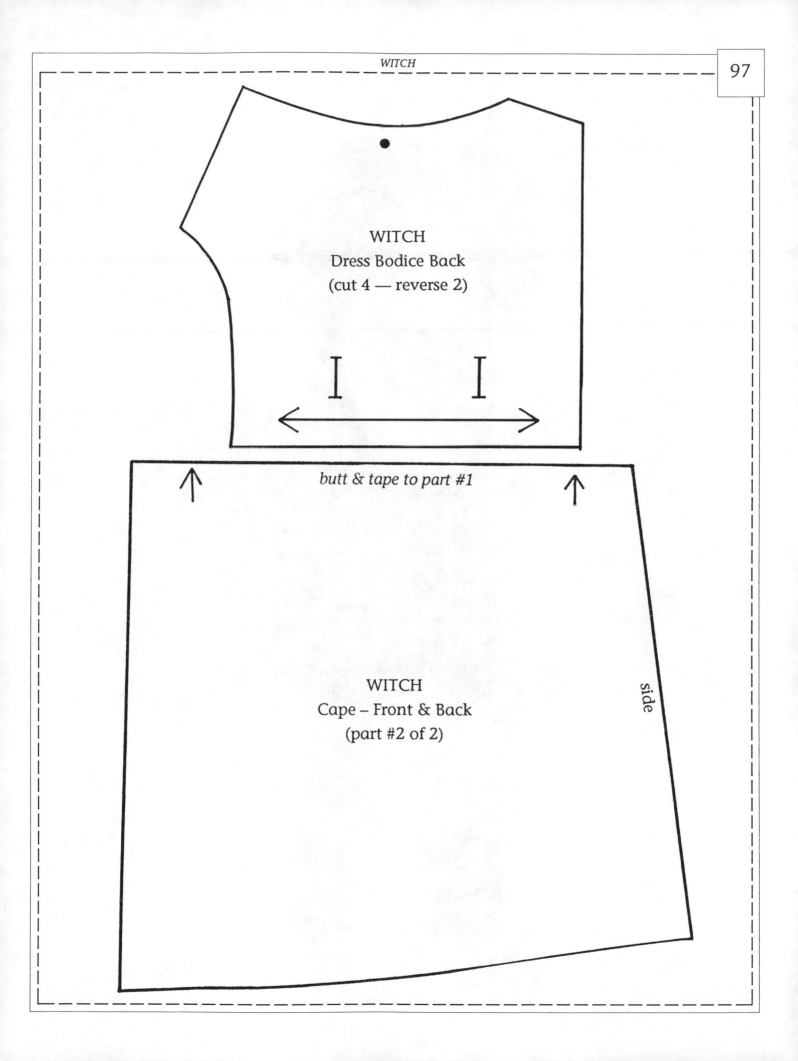

WITCH
Dress Bodice Back
(cut 4 — reverse 2)

butt & tape to part #1

WITCH
Cape – Front & Back
(part #2 of 2)

side

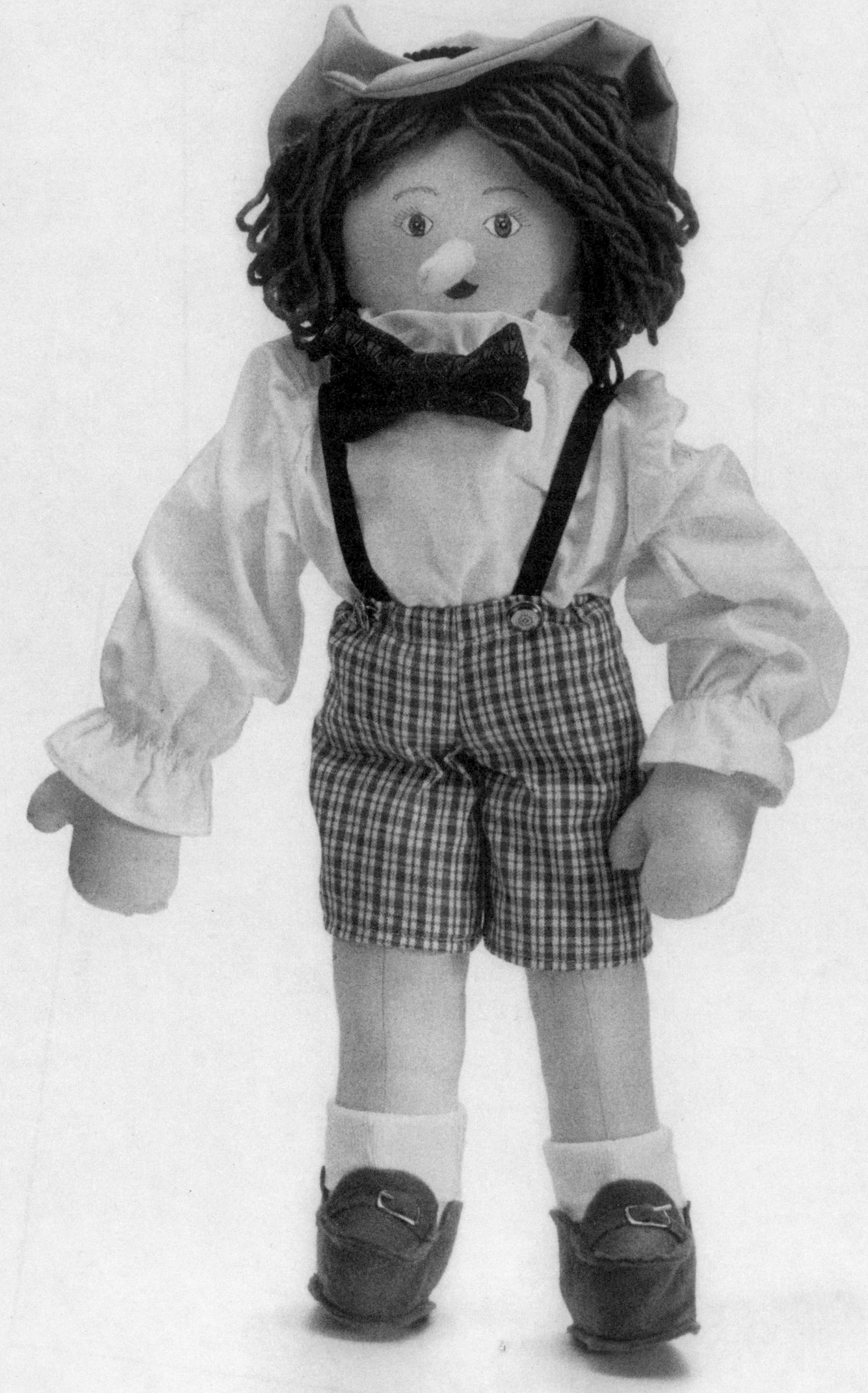

♥

Pinocchio

Ready for mischief, Pinocchio will bring good cheer to children and adults alike. Use muslin for the body, or a beige, patterned fabric to simulate the wood Pinocchio was carved from. You may even add strings to make Pinocchio a real marionette.

To make the doll, follow the instructions for the doll body on page 16. Don't draw a nose on Pinocchio's face. At the beginning of the instructions for Pinocchio, you will find instructions for Pinocchio's nose.

♥

1/4 yard shirt fabric (I used white cotton)

Matching thread

1/4 yard shorts fabric (I used a red plaid)

Matching thread

Scrap of tie fabric (I used a blue paisley)

Matching thread

1/2 yard 3/8"-wide black grograin ribbon for suspenders

Four 1/2" buttons

White ribbing or knit fabric for socks

One piece of brown felt

Matching thread

Small gold buckles

3/8 yard hat fabric (I used blue)

1/2 yard 1/4"-wide black roping-like trim for hat

Two or three feathers for the hat

Brown yarn for the hair
(I used 1/4 of a skein)

Matching thread

INSTRUCTIONS

Turn to page 16 for instructions for the doll body. Make the doll and paint or embroider the face, excluding the nose. Then, return here and make Pinocchio's nose, outfit, and hair.

Prepare the pattens and cut and mark the fabric as instructed in the Basics. Cut one tie piece 6½" x 5" and one tie center 1½" x 2".

Note: All seam allowances are ¼" unless directed otherwise.

Nose

1. Lay the nose pattern on a piece of the body fabric and trace around it. Place this marked piece, markings up, on another piece of body fabric. Stitch just inside the marked line, as shown, leaving the short, straight line unstitched. Trim to within ⅛" of the stitching and across the short, straight marked line.

Turn right side out. Stuff. Turn the raw edges at the opening to the inside. Stitch to the face.

Shirt

1. Stitch the two shirt pieces together at one shoulder.

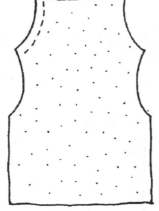

2. Press ³/₄" at neck edge of shirt down to wrong side of shirt. Cut a piece of elastic 6" long. Pin one end of the elastic over the raw edge, having the end of the elastic even with the raw side edge of the shirt. Repeat for the other end of the elastic. Zigzag stitch the elastic in place, over the raw edge of the turned up bottom edge of the shirt neck, holding the ends of the elastic firmly and stretching the elastic as you sew.

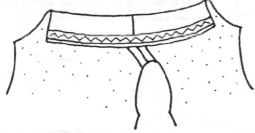

3. Right sides facing, stitch the second shirt shoulder seam.

4. Press 1" at the bottom edge of each sleeve to the wrong side. Cut two pieces of elastic 4" long each. Apply as you did for the neck.

5. Gather stitch the top edge of the sleeve. Match the dots on the sleeves to the dots on the shirt. Pin. Pull up on the gather threads. Adjust gathers. Pin. Stitch. Repeat for the second sleeve.

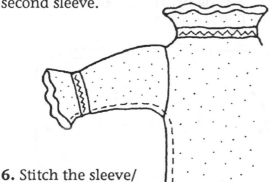

6. Stitch the sleeve/ side seams.

7. Press under ¹/₄" at hem edge of shirt. Repeat. Topstitch.

Shorts

1. Right sides together, fold one shorts piece in half the same way you cut it out. Stitch the inside leg seam. Repeat for the other shorts piece.

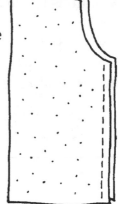

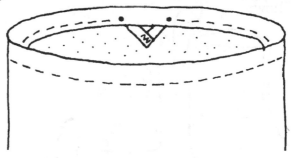

2. Turn one shorts piece right side out. Put it inside the other shorts piece, which is still wrong side out (right sides are thus facing). Match the long curved crotch seam. Stitch.

3. Turn shorts right side out. Press under ¹/₄" on the top edge. Press under ¹/₂". Topstitch along the bottom fold, leaving a ¹/₂"- wide gap in the stitching for inserting elastic.

4. Cut a piece of elastic 9" long. Attach a safety pin to each end. Insert one safety pin into the casing. Work it all the way around and push it back out the opening. Overlap the ends of the elastic ¹/₂". Stitch them together.

5. Press ¹/₄" to the wrong side along the hem edge of both pants legs. Repeat. Topstitch.

6. Put the shorts on the doll. Cut the suspender ribbon into two pieces. Stitch the ends to the back of the top edge of the shorts as shown, 1" from the center seam of the shorts. Sew buttons to the front of the shorts.

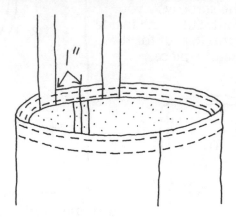

Socks

1. Right sides facing, stitch two sock pieces together, leaving the top, straight edges unstitched.

Turn right side out. Put on doll. Fold down as shown.

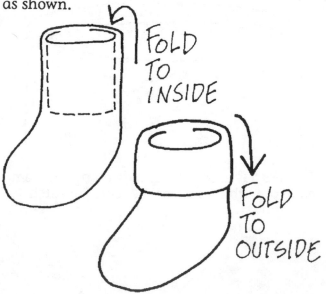

Shoes

Note: All seams for the shoes are 1/8" and face to the outside.

1. Stitch the shoe side piece together at the center back seam.

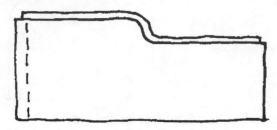

2. Stitch the shoe top to the shoe sides as shown. Begin and end the stitching at the dots on the shoe top.

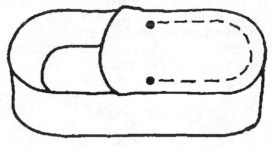

3. Stitch the shoe bottom to the remaining raw edge of the shoe side.

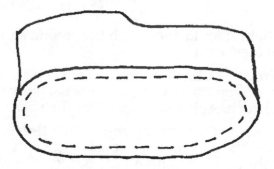

4. Cut a 1/4"-wide strip of felt. Put the buckle on it. Stitch to the shoe.

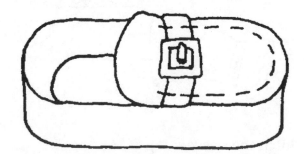

Bow Tie

1. Right sides facing, fold the $6\frac{1}{2}$" x 5" tie piece together so that it measures $6\frac{1}{2}$" x $2\frac{1}{2}$". Stitch around the raw edges, leaving a $\frac{1}{2}$"-wide opening for turning as shown.

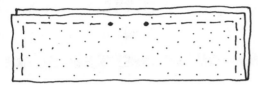

2. Hold the smaller tie piece (tie center) so that the $1\frac{1}{2}$" is horizontal. Fold the side edges toward the center so that they meet and wrong sides match.

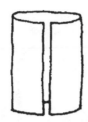

Fold the tie as shown. Pinch the middle, and wrap the tie center around the middle of the tie. Tack at the back. From inside the shirt, safety pin the tie to the center front of the shirt at the elastic.

Hair

1. Draw a 3"-long line on a piece of paper. Put the top of the line on the paper under the presser foot of your sewing machine.

2. Wind the yarn around your fingers so that the loops are 8" wide.

3. Lay the center of the yarn across the line on the paper. Stitch through the centers of the lengths of the hair to the paper, filling the 3" evenly. Backstitch at the beginning and ends of the stitching.

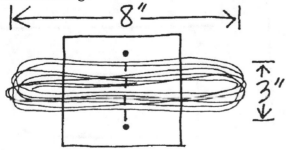

Tear away the paper.

4. Place the wig in the doll's head, with the seam as a "part" in the hair. Hand stitch in place. To keep the hair from falling in the doll's face, apply a little thinned glue to the top sides of the face. Press the hair to the glue.

Hat

1. Right sides facing, stitch the two hat pieces together. Cut a 2"-long slash in the middle of one hat piece (to be underside of hat.) Turn right side out. Press.

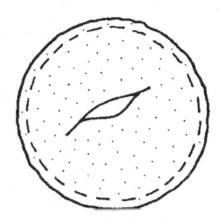

2. Gather stitch $1\frac{1}{2}$" from the edge of the hat. Pull up on the gathers. Tie the threads. Put the hat on the doll. Tie the rope in a knot around the brim of the hat. Tack over the gather stitching. Glue or tack the feathers in place.

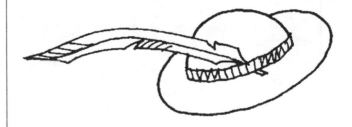

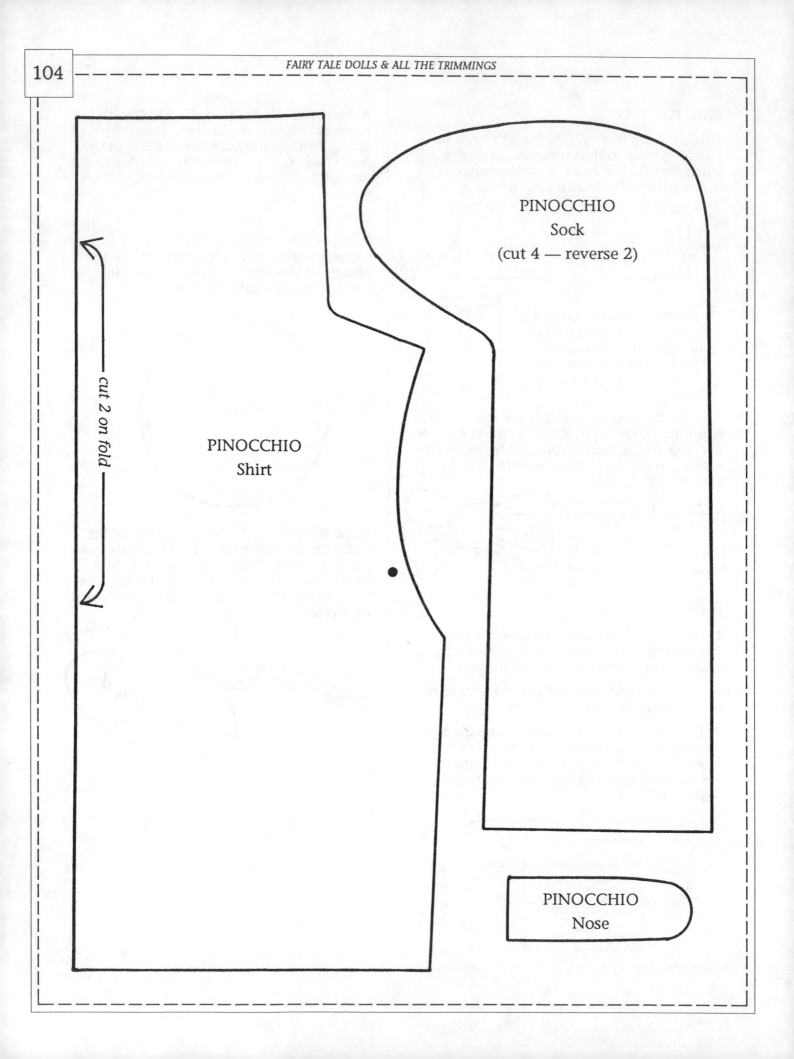

PINOCCHIO
Sock
(cut 4 — reverse 2)

cut 2 on fold

PINOCCHIO
Shirt

PINOCCHIO
Nose

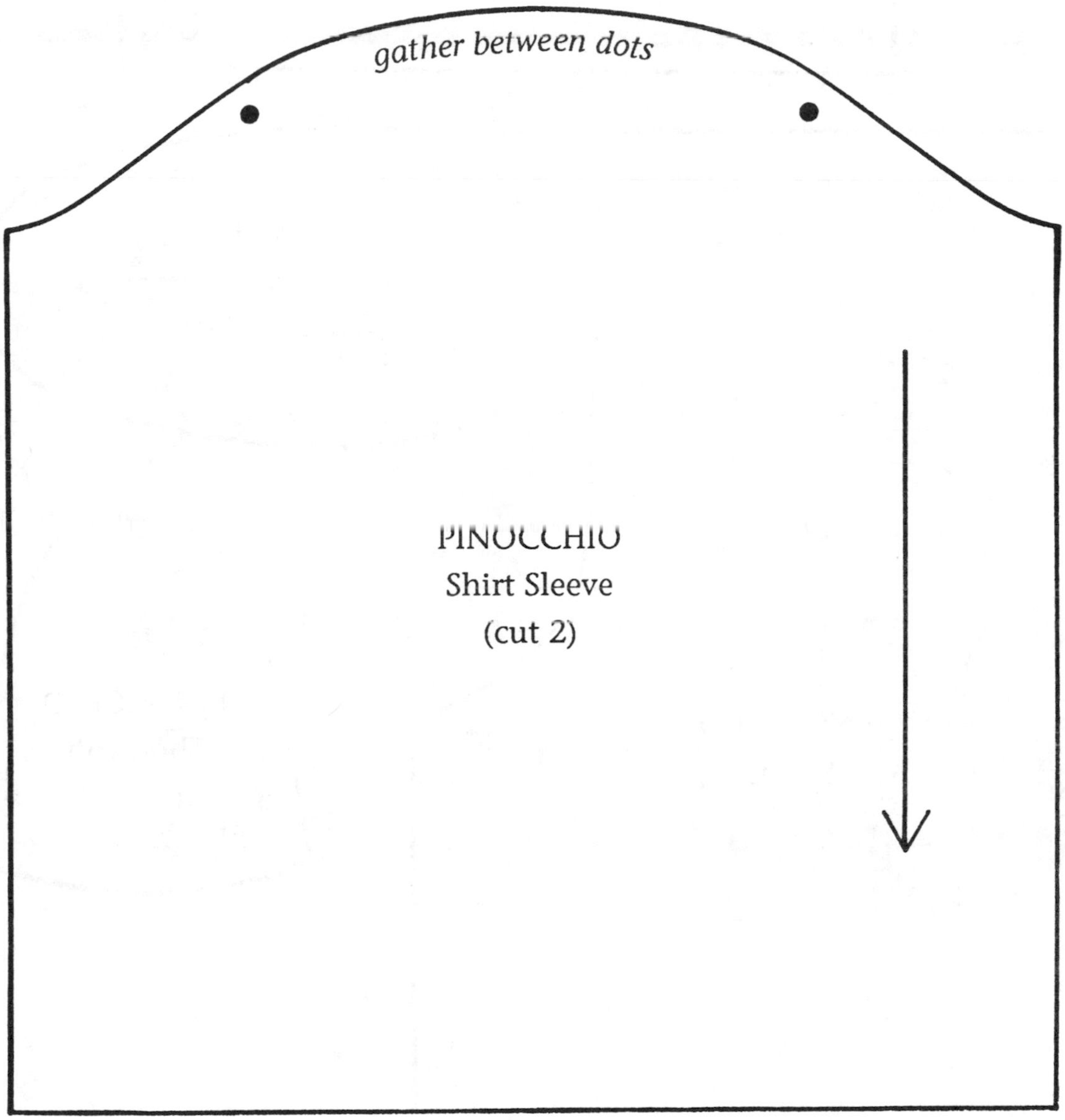

gather between dots

PINOCCHIO
Shirt Sleeve
(cut 2)

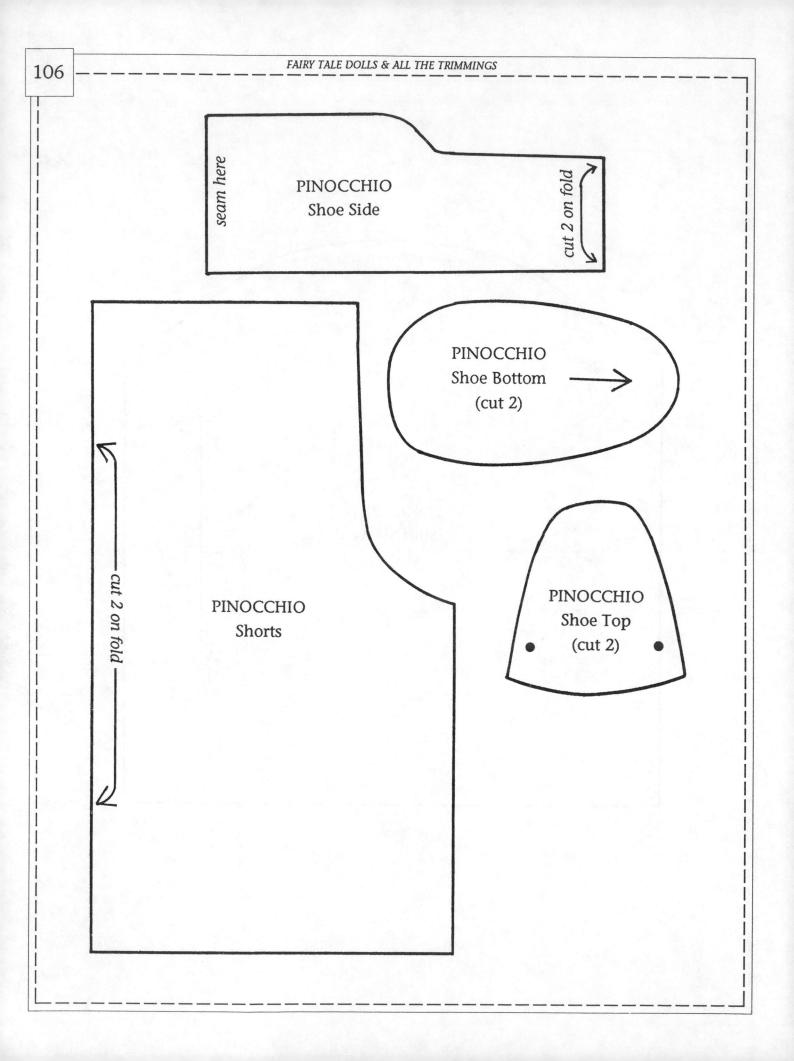

PINOCCHIO
Shoe Side

seam here

cut 2 on fold

PINOCCHIO
Shoe Bottom
(cut 2)

PINOCCHIO
Shorts

cut 2 on fold

PINOCCHIO
Shoe Top
(cut 2)

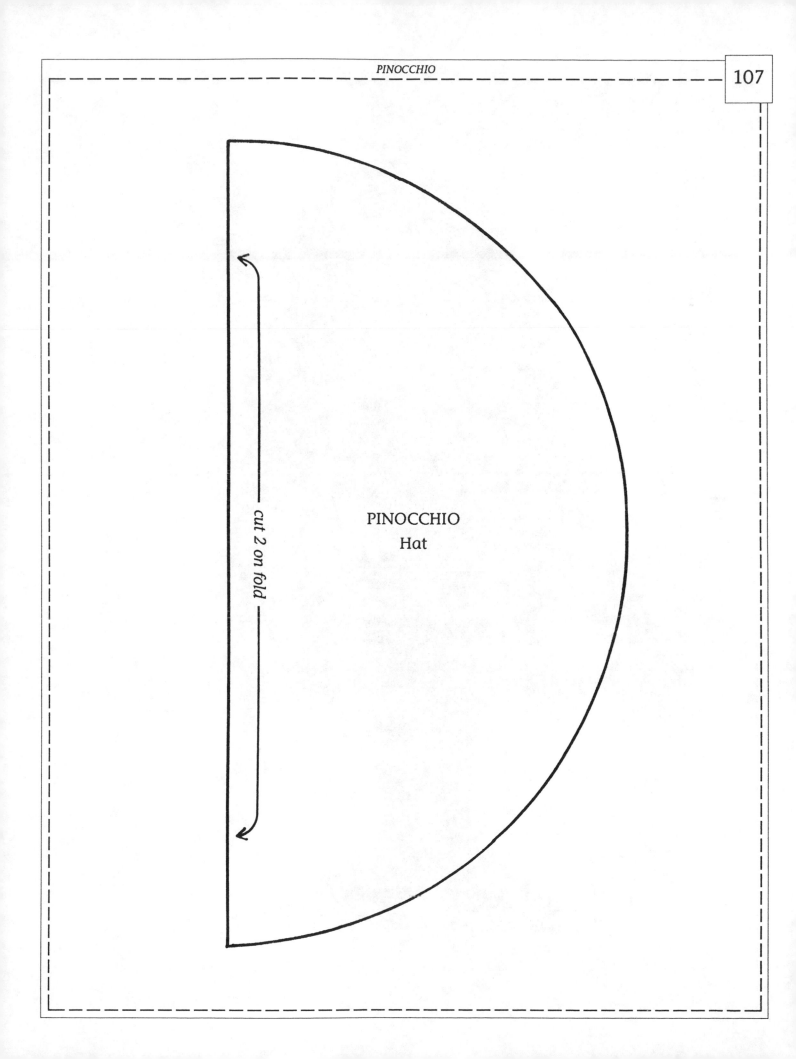

cut 2 on fold

PINOCCHIO
Hat

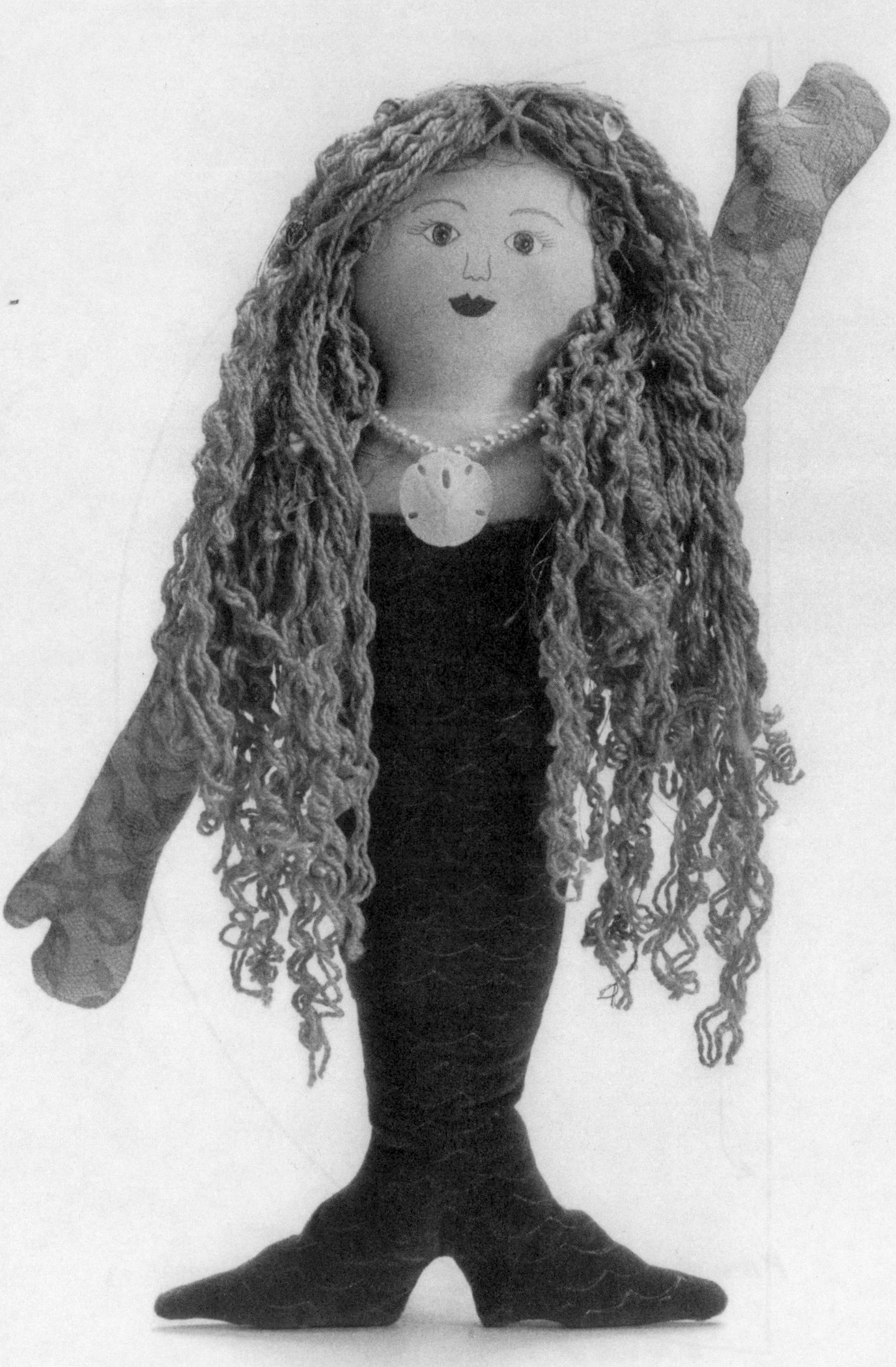

♥

The Little Mermaid

This doll is made from the same character doll body used with the previous dolls but with a slight variation. She has no legs. Rather, her tail is one with her head/body. You'll find complete instructions on the following pages.

♥

I used green velvet for The Little Mermaid's body. Velveteen, fine-wale corduroy or green doe suede will work just as well. The scales are embroidered with metallic thread. This is easy to use. Simply use normal thread in the bobbin and the metallic thread in the needle. My sewing machine has a wonderful built-in scallop stitch that proved perfect for her scales. In case your machine lacks this feature, I have provided a scale template. To use it, lay a piece of stabilizer or waxed paper over the template and trace the design onto it. Repeat until the scale pattern is large enough to cover the velvet body. Then you can pin the stabilizer or waxed paper over the velveteen in step 3, stitch, and tear the paper away.

The doll's gloves are simply lace fabric. I chose one with decoratively finished selvedges so I didn't have to finish the top of the gloves.

Three different yarns are listed for The Little Mermaid's hair. The first is the yellow/gold. The last two contribute blue/green and brown highlights in her hair, appropriate for her oceanic origins. Depending upon the end use of your doll, you may or may not wish to use these extra yarns. Therefore, I have listed them as optional.

MATERIALS

⅓ yard muslin
Matching thread
⅓ yard green velvet
Matching thread
Gold metallic thread
Tear-away stabilizer
Polyester fiberfill stuffing
½ yard lace fabric (see above)
Prestrung 6mm pearls
Assorted shells
Craft Glue
Acrylic craft paints
1 skein yarn (I used Moon Beams shade 8530 amber)
Matching thread
Optional yarns: colors shade 9506 Jade Stone by Yarns Brunswick; fur, color Bagno by Baruffa

INSTRUCTIONS

Turn to the Basics and follow the instructions for dyeing the fabric (if desired) and preparing the patterns. You will find the body and arm patterns on page 18 and 19.

Note: A short machine stitch of 1.5 or 8 to 10 stitches to the inch, will make stronger seams and ease stitching around tight curves.

Note: Seam allowances for all body patterns in this book are not included on the pattern pieces. You will stitch on the traced lines and cut the pieces out after stitching. This is a much more accurate method to construct the dolls.

1. Cut two pieces of muslin approximately 10" x 19". Cut a piece of stabilizer 10" x 14".

2. Trace the front body pattern onto the velvet. Trace the back body pattern, leaving at least an inch of space between the two pattern pieces where they come close together. Cut them apart so you will have two pieces of fabric with a design traced on each piece.

If you need to mark the scalloped scale lines (see introduction), do so now.

3.. Right side up, lay one piece of velvet on top of one of the muslin rectangles you cut out in step 1. Pin the velvet to the muslin. If you are using a scale stitching template, pin on velvet. Slip the stabilizer under the muslin. Pin all three layers together.

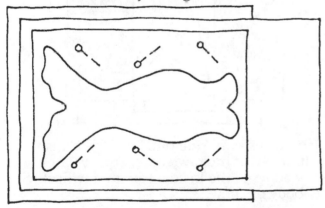

Using metallic thread, machine stitch the scales in horizontal rows across the doll's body. Satin stitch what will be the top edge of the green body, still using metallic thread.

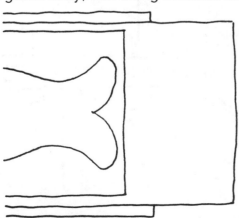

Tear away the stabilizer from the back of the muslin. Tear away scale template if used.

Trim away the extraneous velvet above the satin stitching as shown.

4. Lay the full head/body pattern over the embroidered muslin/velvet. Match up the lines drawn on the velvet with the edges of the pattern. Trace the head/shoulders portion of the doll onto the muslin.

Repeat for the other side (front or back) of the doll.

5. Hold front or back of the doll against a window with the velvet on the glass. Fit the head/body pattern over the doll so it fits in the lines seen when holding fabric up to the light. Trace around the paper pattern so you will have these stitching lines on the back (wrong side) of the muslin.

Hold this side, front or back, of the doll against the other half, velvet sides facing. Match them up as best you can. Starting at any point (I do the head first) on the traced stitching line, push a pin from the line you just marked through the fabric and through the corresponding place on the line on the other side.

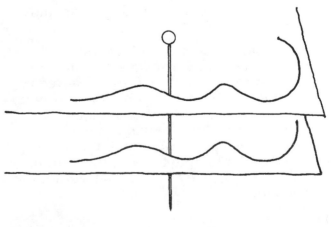

I do two points like this adjacent to one another and then put a pin in the fabric between them in the normal way. I work around the doll like this until it is all pinned.

Stitch along the stitching line through all layers. Leave a 2"-wide opening in the stitching at one side for turning and stuffing.

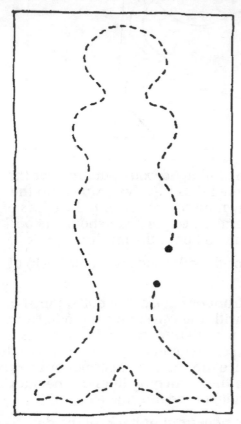

Trim the seam allowances to $1/8$". Apply Fray Check™ to the raw edges of the velvet. Turn right side out. Stuff. Ladder stitch the opening closed.

6. Lay the arm pattern on the muslin and trace around it. Repeat for the second arm, leaving an inch or more between them. Cut them out, leaving a half inch or more outside of the traced lines.

7. Right sides together, fold the lace and insert it between the two layers of one marked arm. Line up the finished selvedges of the lace so they will be about half way up the upper arm. Stitch one arm along the traced stitching lines, leaving the top, straight edge open. Trim the seam allowances to $1/8$". Clip into the V at the thumb. Apply a drop of Fray Check™. Repeat for the second arm.

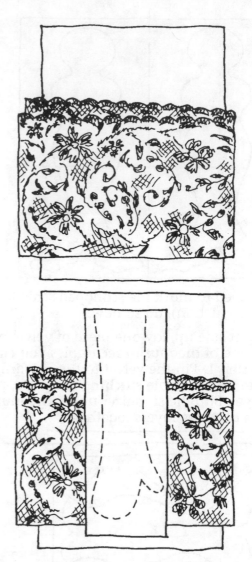

Turn arms right side out. Stuff the arms to within $3/4$" of the raw edges. Turn $1/4$" at the raw edges to the inside. Fold and whipstitch to body as shown.

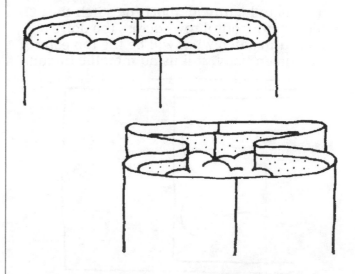

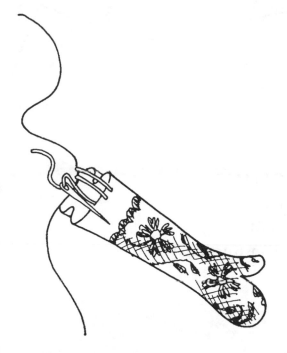

8. Curl the hair by wrapping doubled strands of yarn on metal shish kabob skewers or metal knitting needles. Tape each end of the yarn to secure. Wet the yarn under the faucet. Set it in a 200°F oven until thoroughly dry. Put aside to cool before removing the hair from the skewers. Do this for all of the gold yarn. On about eight skewers of gold yarn add the blue green yarn as a third strand.

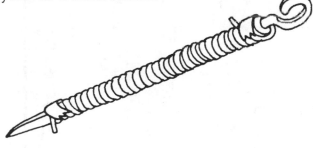

Cut the yarn into roughly 24" lengths. Lay the strands out side by side as shown. If desired, add strands of the Baruffa yarn.

Tie the middle of the wig together with a piece of yarn.

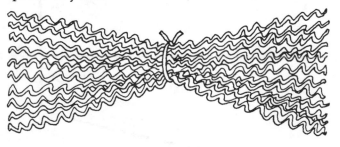

Hold the wig over the head, centering the middle tie at the middle top of the head. Stitch the center of the wig to the head.

Glue small shells in the hair randomly.

Tie prestrung pearls around the neck. Sew a small sand dollar to the necklace with white thread using a hole in the sand dollar to attach it. Glue a starfish or special shell as a crowning gem on the hair above the center of the doll's forehead.

Lift up the hair from the back of the head and spread a thin coating of watered down glue to the muslin. Press the hair in place. To keep the hair at the front from falling in the doll's face, apply the watered down glue to the upper sides of her face over the stitching and on the very top sides of her forehead. Press the hair to the doll's head.

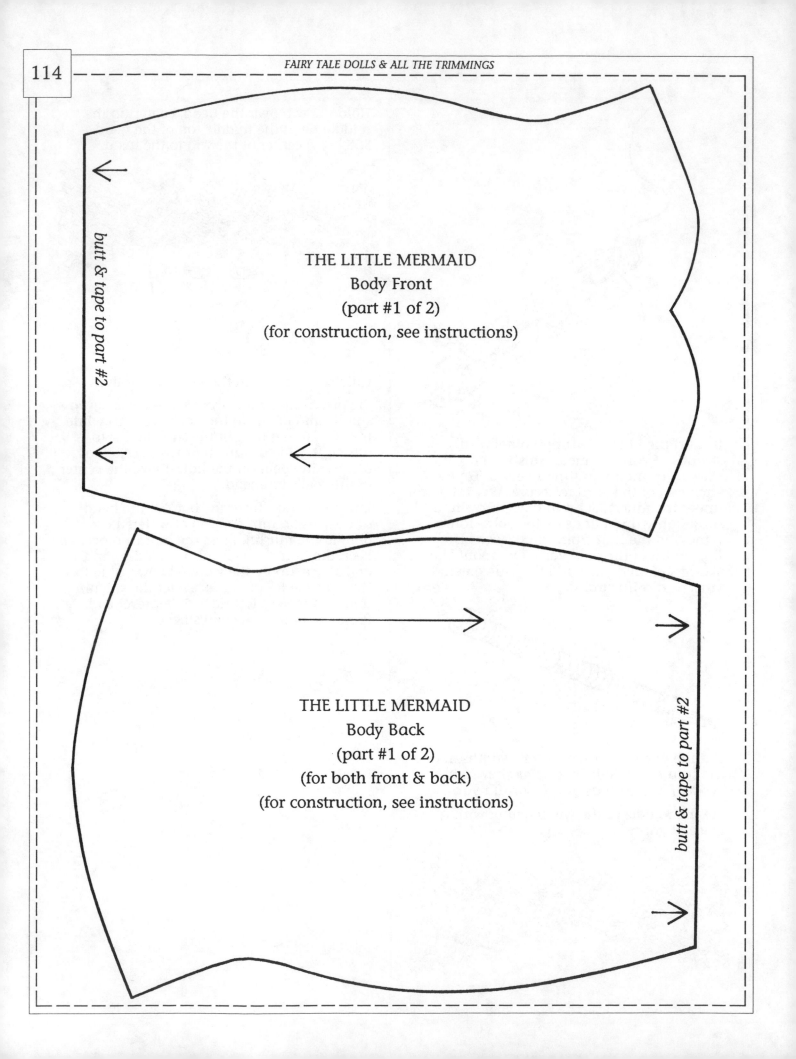

butt & tape to part #2

THE LITTLE MERMAID
Body Front
(part #1 of 2)
(for construction, see instructions)

THE LITTLE MERMAID
Body Back
(part #1 of 2)
(for both front & back)
(for construction, see instructions)

butt & tape to part #2

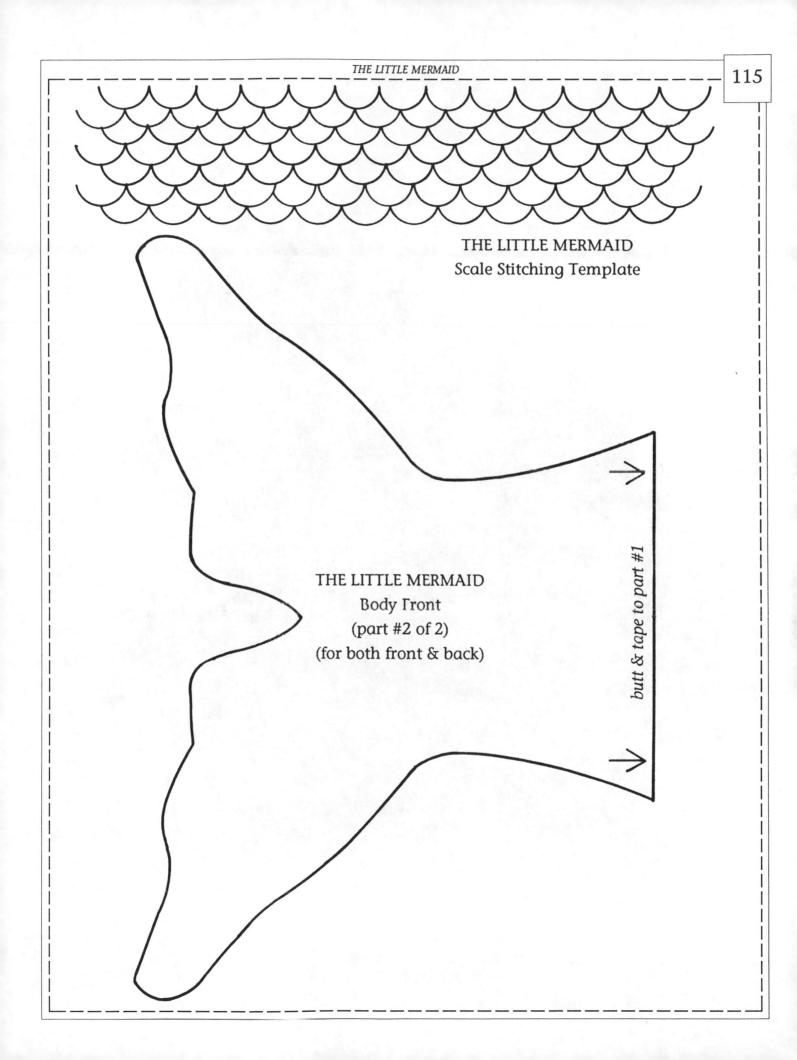

THE LITTLE MERMAID
Scale Stitching Template

THE LITTLE MERMAID
Body Front
(part #2 of 2)
(for both front & back)

butt & tape to part #1

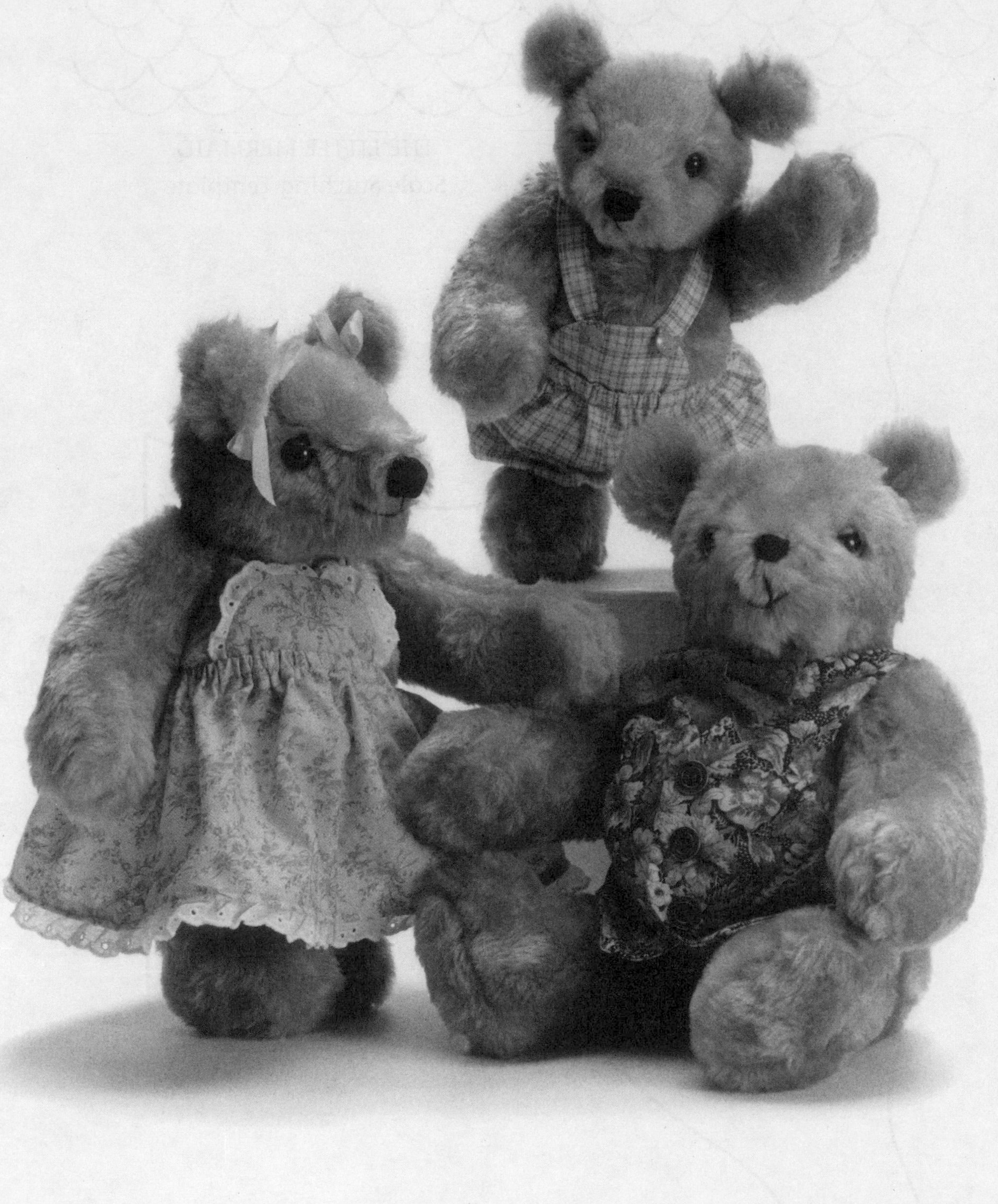

♥

The Three Bears

Goldilocks has no reason to fear these furry bruins. In fact, given the opportunity, they would gladly invite her in for porridge!

Jointed teddy bears are not difficult to make. The sewing is easy — just simple shapes. Fur fabric presents no problems; just switch to a size 14 or 16 needle.

♥

Papa Bear stands 14" tall, Mama 12¹/₂" tall, and Baby Bear 11¹/₂" tall.

MATERIALS

Synthetic fur fabric (see Sources):

³/₈ yard for Papa Bear

¹/₃ yard for Mama Bear

¹/₄ yard for Baby Bear or 1 yard for all three bears

Matching thread

Plastic teddy bear joint sets:

Five 40 mm for Papa Bear

Five 35 mm for Mama Bear

Five 30 mm for Baby Bear

Safety eyes:

Two 14 mm for Papa Bear

Two 12 mm for Mama Bear

Two 12 mm for Baby Bear

Waxed dental floss, or quilting or carpet thread for hand sewing seams

Black pearl cotton or embroidery floss

Polyester fiberfill stuffing

Papa Bear's Vest and Bow Tie

¹/₄ yard fabric for vest

Matching thread

¹/₄ yard fabric for bow tie

¹/₃ yard ¹/₂"-wide black elastic

Mama Bear's Jumper

¹/₄ yard fabric

Matching thread

1 yard ¹/₂"-wide gathered eyelet

¹/₂ yard ¹/₄"-wide elastic

¹/₂ yard ⁵/₈"-wide ribbon for ties

Baby Bear's Romper

¹/₄ yard fabric

Matching thread

¹/₂ yard ¹/₄"-wide elastic

¹/₂ yard ⁵/₈"-wide ribbon for ties

Two ¹/₂" – ³/₄" buttons

INSTRUCTIONS

Note: All seam allowances are ¹/₄" unless otherwise instructed and are included in the bear and clothing patterns.

The Bears

Prepare the patterns as instructed in the Basics.

1. Stroke the fur as you would a dog. Lay the fur fabric fur side down on your work surface so that the nap of the fur points toward you (as if you were standing behind the dog). Lay the pattern pieces on the fabric with the arrows pointing toward you. Trace around them. Check to be sure you have traced the appropriate number of each pattern piece and have flipped them over as indicated to make a right and a left arm, for instance.

Cut out the fur pieces on the inside of the traced lines. Transfer all markings.

2. Right sides facing, pin the two body front pieces together along the center front seam.

3. Right sides facing, pin the two body back pieces together along the center back seam. Stitch from the top to the first dot. Stitch from the bottom dot down to the bottom. The gap left in the stitching between the two dots will provide access into the body for turning the body right side out and for installing the head, arm, and leg joints. This opening will be at the bear's center back.

4. Right sides facing, pin the body fronts to the body backs (check the nap to see which way is up), matching the double notches. Starting from one dot at the top, stitch the body fronts to the body backs, down one side and up the other. Stop at the second dot. This will leave an opening for the head joint post.

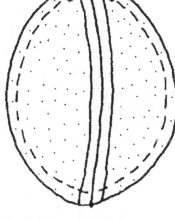

5. Fold one arm in half, right sides facing. Stitch, leaving a gap in the stitching between the dots, as shown. Repeat for the second arm.

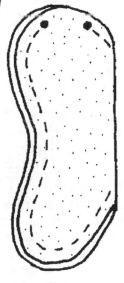

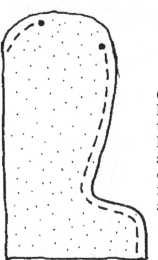

6. Fold one leg in half, right sides together. Stitch, leaving the bottom, straight edges open and leaving a gap in the stitching as shown.

Right sides facing, pin a foot pad to the bottom edge of one foot. Match the dot to the seam at the back of the foot. Place the leg under the presser foot of your sewing machine so that the foot pad is against the sole plate. Stitch.

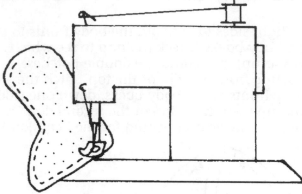

Repeat for the second leg.

7. Right sides facing, pin the two head side pieces together along the chin. Stitch from the nose down to the bottom of the neck.

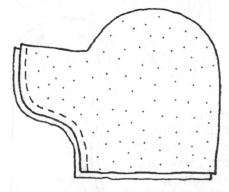

Right sides facing, pin the dot on the head gusset to the seam where the two head sides meet at the nose. Pin one side of the head gusset to one head side from the nose to the bottom of the neck, easing the head gusset to fit. Stitch. Repeat for the other side of the head gusset/head side.

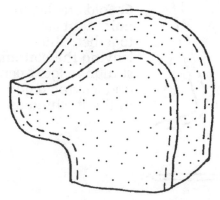

8. Right sides facing, pin and stitch the curved edges of two ear pieces together. Repeat for the other two ear pieces.

9. Make holes at the eye markings in the head. Turn the head right side out. Push the post of one eye into the bear's head, through the hole. From inside the head, snap a metal lockwasher onto the eye post. If you have trouble, put the head eye down on a padded surface. Use a spool of thread to push the lockwasher on the post, centering the hole in the spool over the post.

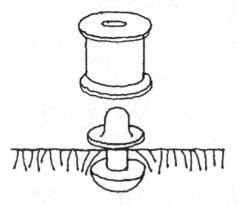

10. To stuff the head, start at the nose with walnut-size pieces of fiberfill. Use the handle of a wooden spoon to force the fiberfill firmly into the nose. Repeat several times. Continue stuffing the head with handfuls of stuffing, pushing it in with the spoon. Stop stuffing when you have stuffed to about 1/2" from the raw edges at the bottom neck opening.

Thread a needle with the dental floss or heavy thread. With the head upside down, gather stitch the neck opening as shown. Go around once. Lay the flat side of a stationary disk on the stuffing in the neck opening. Pull up on the gathering stitches. Continue stitching around the neck opening, going once or twice more around, pulling up every stitch or two. When the raw edges are gathered around the post, knot the thread.

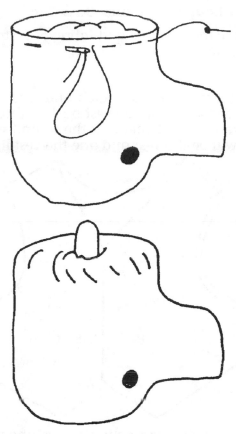

Put stationary disks inside each of the arms and legs, pointing the posts out of the holes. For each limb in turn, push the post into the body through the respective hole. Remember that the opening in the body is at the center back. Make sure that the legs and arms point in the proper directions. Slide a large washer onto the post. Snap a lockwasher on. Push all the way down.

To tighten the joints, find a socket from a socket wrench set or two large nuts (need two for height) that will fit around the post and are taller than it. Lay the bear down on the floor so that the flat part of the joint faces the floor. Put the socket or washers over the post and pound the joint tight with a hammer.

To make the joints extra secure, find some metal lockwashers that are supplied with safety eyes that are large enough to fit on the posts. Hammer these in place.

13. Stuff the bear. Ladder stitch the openings closed.

14. Embroider the nose and mouth as illustrated.

11. Push the post that protrudes from the neck into the gap left in the stitching at the top of the body. From inside the body, slide the large plastic washer onto the post. Next, snap the small plastic lockwasher onto the post. Push down until you hear it snap on.

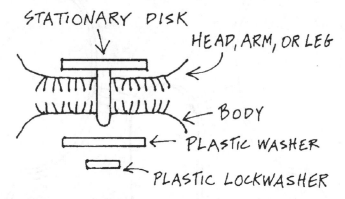

12. Find the dots you marked on the arms and legs. Make holes with a seam ripper or awl at the dots. These need to be large enough for the post of the joint to go through.

Find the dots marked inside the body. Make holes there also.

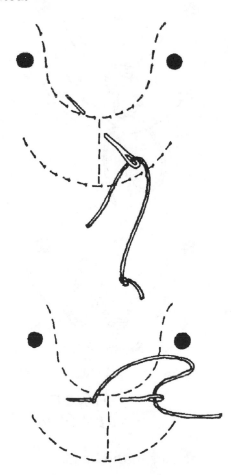

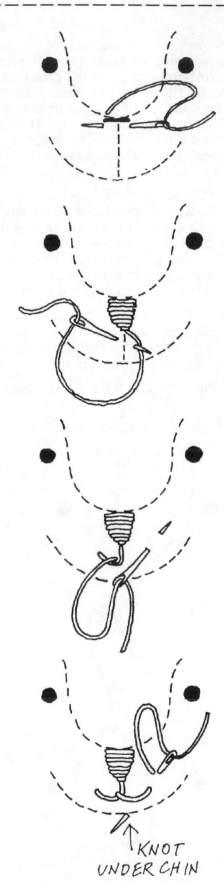

KNOT UNDER CHIN

15. Sew the ears to the head.

Papa Bear's Vest and Bow Tie

Prepare the patterns and fabric as instructed in the Basics.

Vest

1. Right sides facing, match and stitch the shoulder seams of one vest back to those of two vest fronts. Repeat for the second set. One will be the vest and one the vest lining.

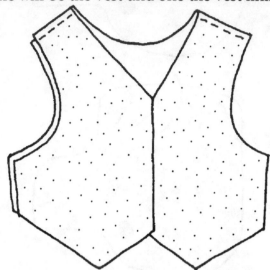

2. Right sides facing, pin the vest and vest facing together. Stitch as shown, leaving the sides open.

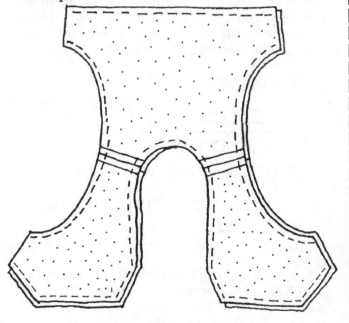

Turn right side out. Press.

3. For each side of the vest, turn the ¼" seam allowance at the front side edge of the vest to the inside. Insert the back side edge inside. Stitch.

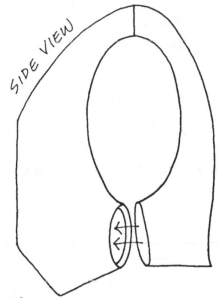

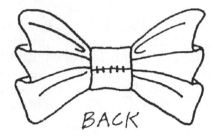

BACK

5. Cut a piece of elastic 11" long. Overlap the ends 1/4". Stitch them together. Stitch to the back of the tie.

Bow Tie

1. Cut a rectangle measuring 8½" x 4". Cut a 2½" square.

2. Fold the rectangle in half lengthwise. Stitch the three raw edges together leaving a 1"-wide opening for turning as shown.

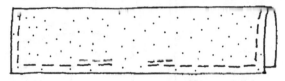

Turn right side out.

3. Fold the square in half. Stitch as shown.

Turn right side out.

4. Fold the tie as shown.

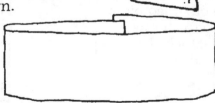

Fold the tie center around the tie as shown and stitch at the back of the tie.

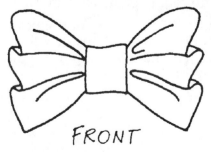

FRONT

Mama Bear's Jumper

Prepare the pattern and fabric as instructed in the Basics. Cut the jumper skirt 6" x 32".

1. Baste the eyelet to the right side of one bib piece.

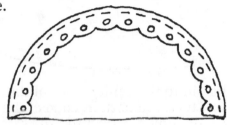

Right sides facing, pin and stitch the two bib pieces together, including the eyelet in the seam. Turn right side out.

2. Match the two short edges of the jumper skirt. Stitch. Press the seam open.

Press under ¼" along one long raw edge of the skirt. Repeat. Topstitch. This will be the hem.

Cut a piece of eyelet 32½" long. Seam the two ends together. Stitch to the hem of the skirt, right side of lace facing wrong side of hem edge.

Press under ¼" on the remaining long raw edge. Press under an additional ½". Topstitch close to the bottom fold, leaving a ½" gap in the stitching for inserting the elastic.

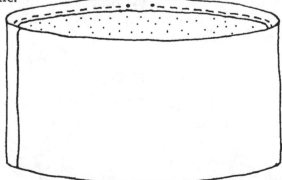

3. Cut a piece of elastic 12" long. Put a safety pin on each end. Push one safety pin into the gap in the casing stitching. Work it all the way around and come out again. Remove the safety pins. Overlap the ends of the elastic ½". Stitch. Stitch the gap in the topstitching closed.

4. Fold the skirt as shown to find the center front. Mark with a pin.

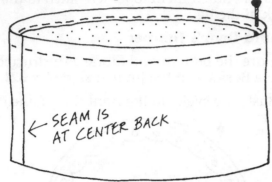

← SEAM IS AT CENTER BACK

Match the pin to the center front of the apron bib. Stitch the bottom edge of the bib to the skirt as shown, stretching the elastic in the skirt a bit to flatten out the gathers in the skirt.

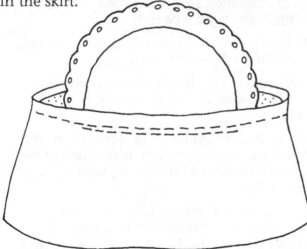

Cut the ribbon in half. Stitch one end of each of the ribbons to the wrong side of the bib as shown. Tie the ribbons in a bow behind the bear's neck.

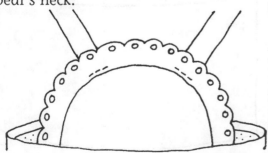

Baby Bear's Romper

Prepare the patterns and fabric as instructed in the Basics.

1. Right sides facing, pin and stitch the two bib pieces together. Turn right side out.

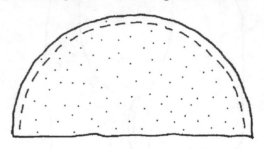

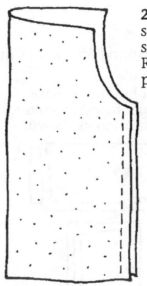

2. Right sides together, stitch the inside legs seam on one leg piece. Repeat for the other leg piece.

3. Turn one leg piece right side out. Put it inside the other leg piece. Match the crotch raw edges. Pin. Stitch. Turn right side out.

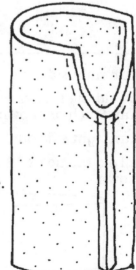

4. Press ¼" to the wrong side at the bottom of each pants leg. Repeat. Topstitch.

5. Press under ¼" at the top of the pants. Press under an additional ½". Topstitch close to the bottom fold, leaving a ½" gap in the stitching for inserting the elastic.

Cut a piece of elastic 12" long. Put a safety pin on each end. Push one safety pin into the gap in the casing stitching. Work it all the way around and come out again. Remove the safety pins. Overlap the ends of the elastic ½". Stitch.

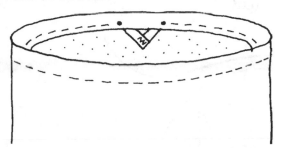

Stitch the gap in the topstitching closed.

6. Match one crotch seam to the middle of the bottom of the apron bib. Stitch the bottom edge of the bib to the pants as shown.

Cut the ribbon in half. Stitch one end of each of the ribbons to the bib as shown. Tie the ribbons in a bow behind the bear's neck.

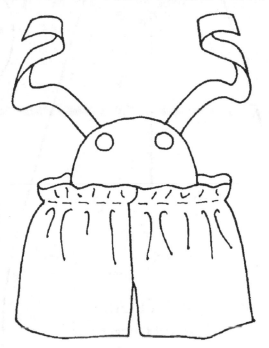

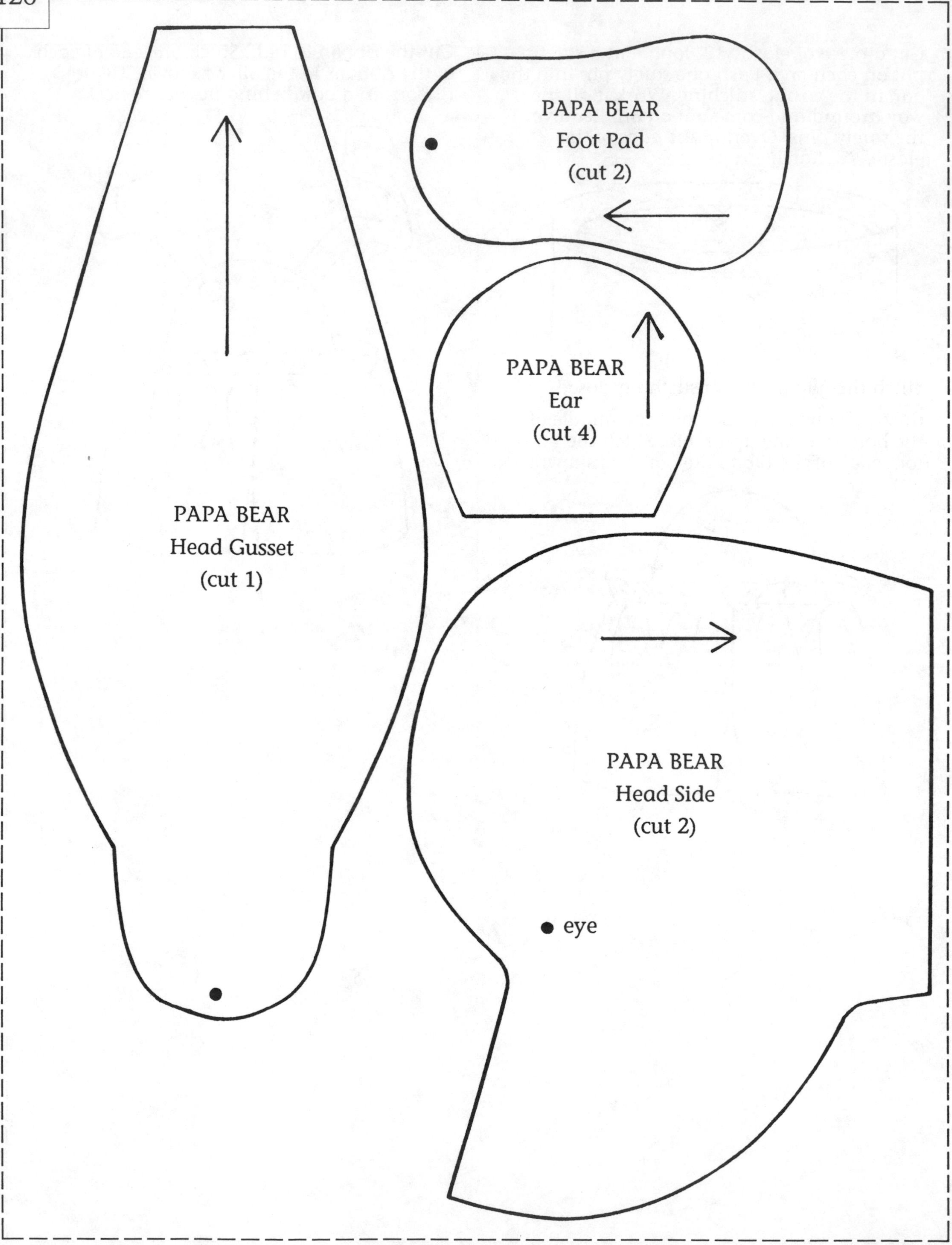

PAPA BEAR
Foot Pad
(cut 2)

PAPA BEAR
Ear
(cut 4)

PAPA BEAR
Head Gusset
(cut 1)

PAPA BEAR
Head Side
(cut 2)

● eye

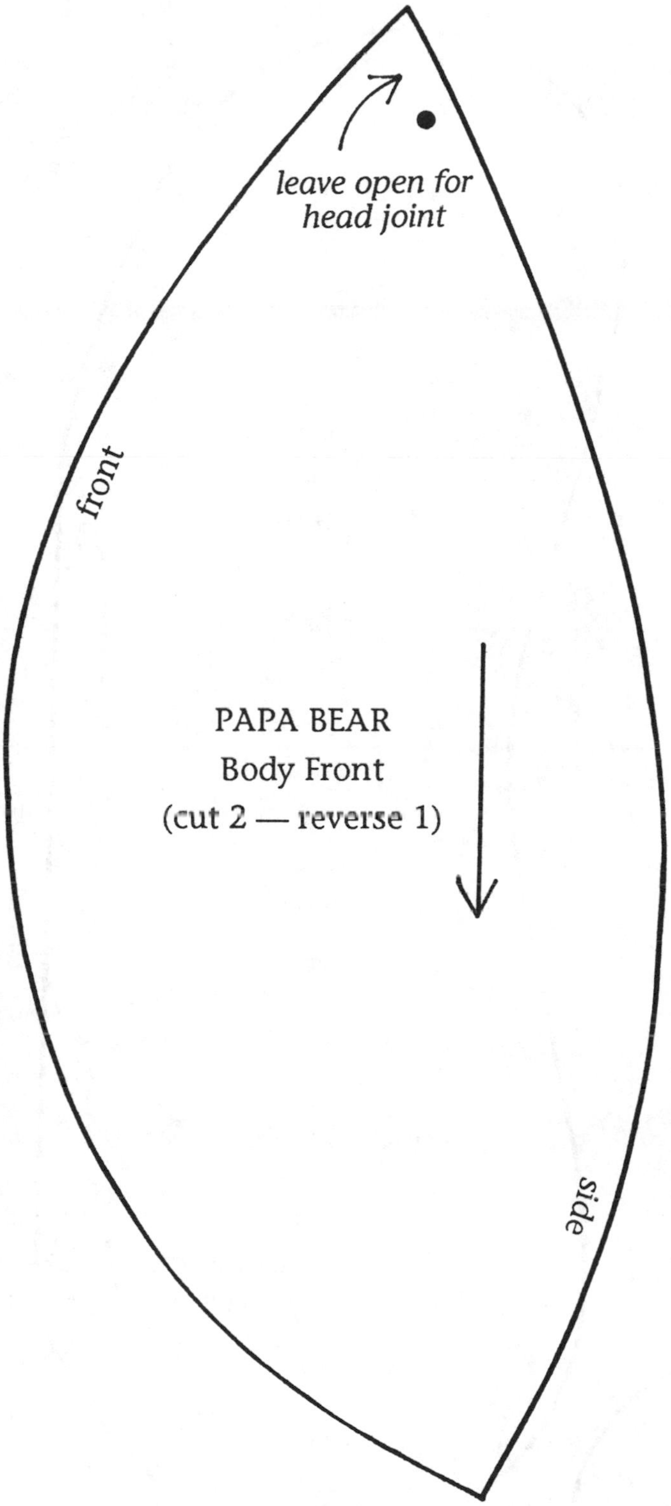

*leave open for
head joint*

front

PAPA BEAR
Body Front
(cut 2 — reverse 1)

side

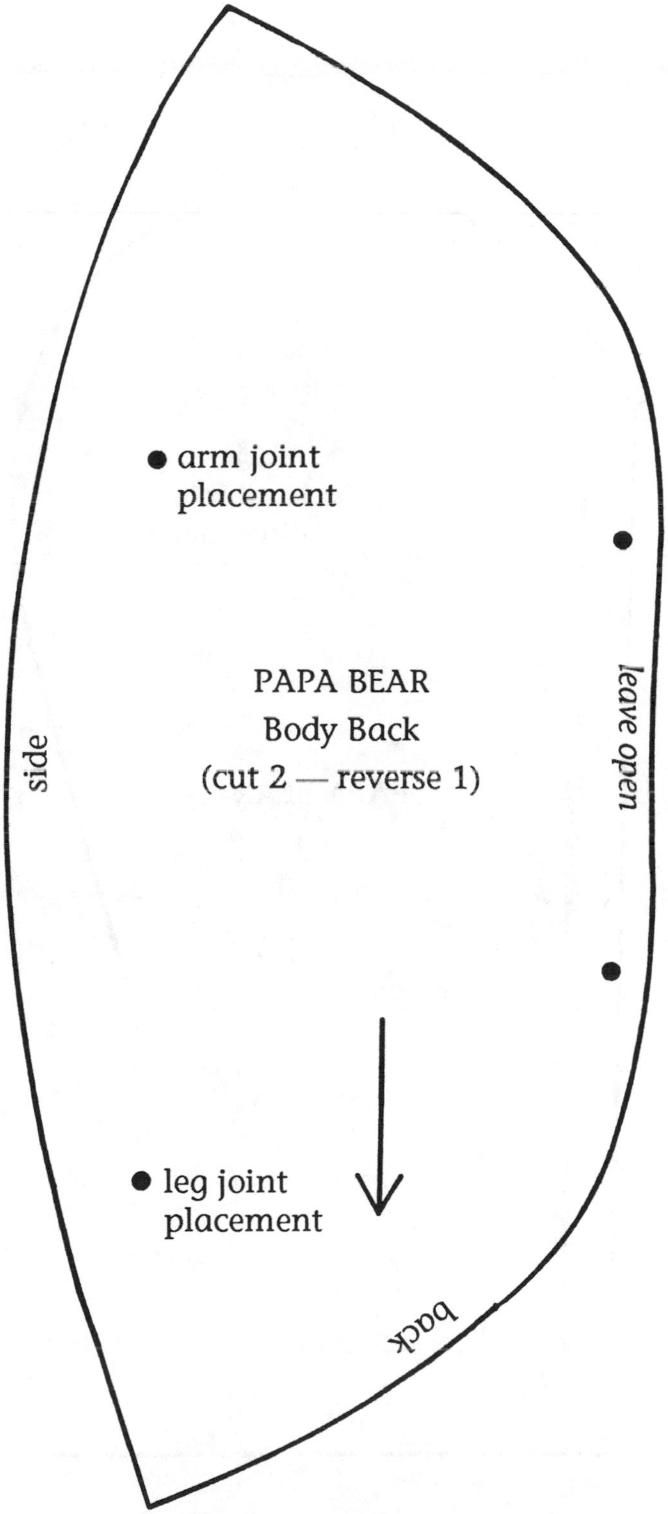

side

• arm joint
placement

PAPA BEAR
Body Back
(cut 2 — reverse 1)

leave open

• leg joint
placement

back

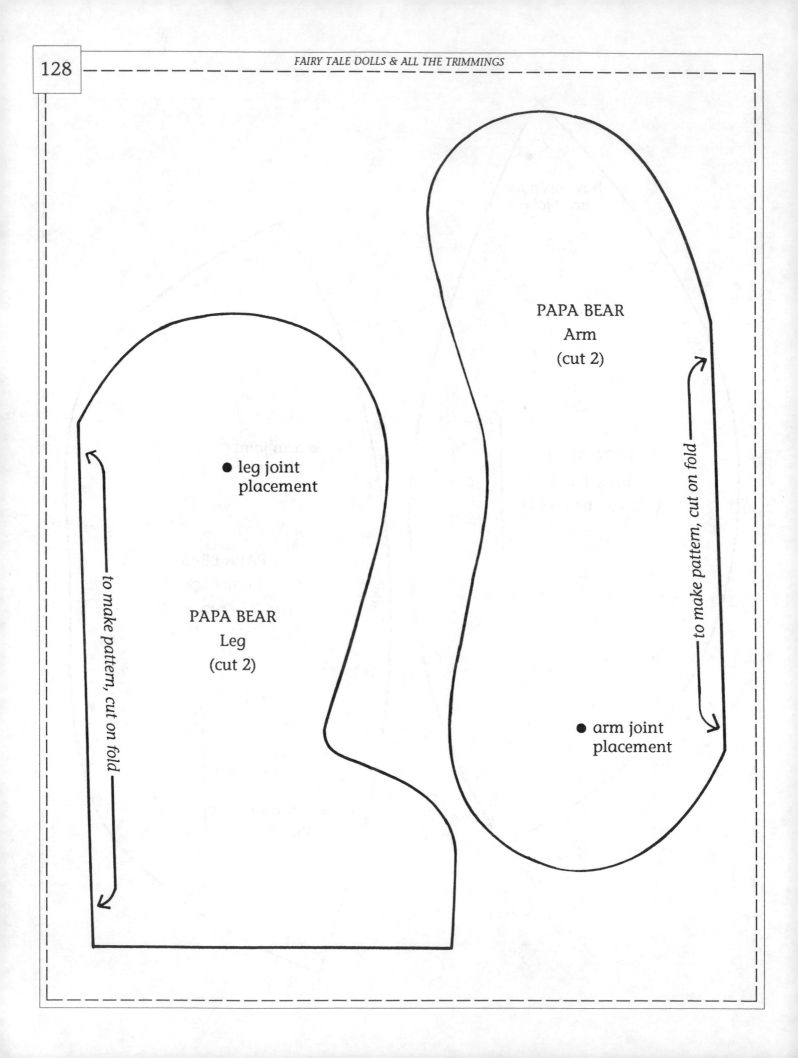

PAPA BEAR
Arm
(cut 2)

to make pattern, cut on fold

● arm joint
placement

● leg joint
placement

PAPA BEAR
Leg
(cut 2)

to make pattern, cut on fold

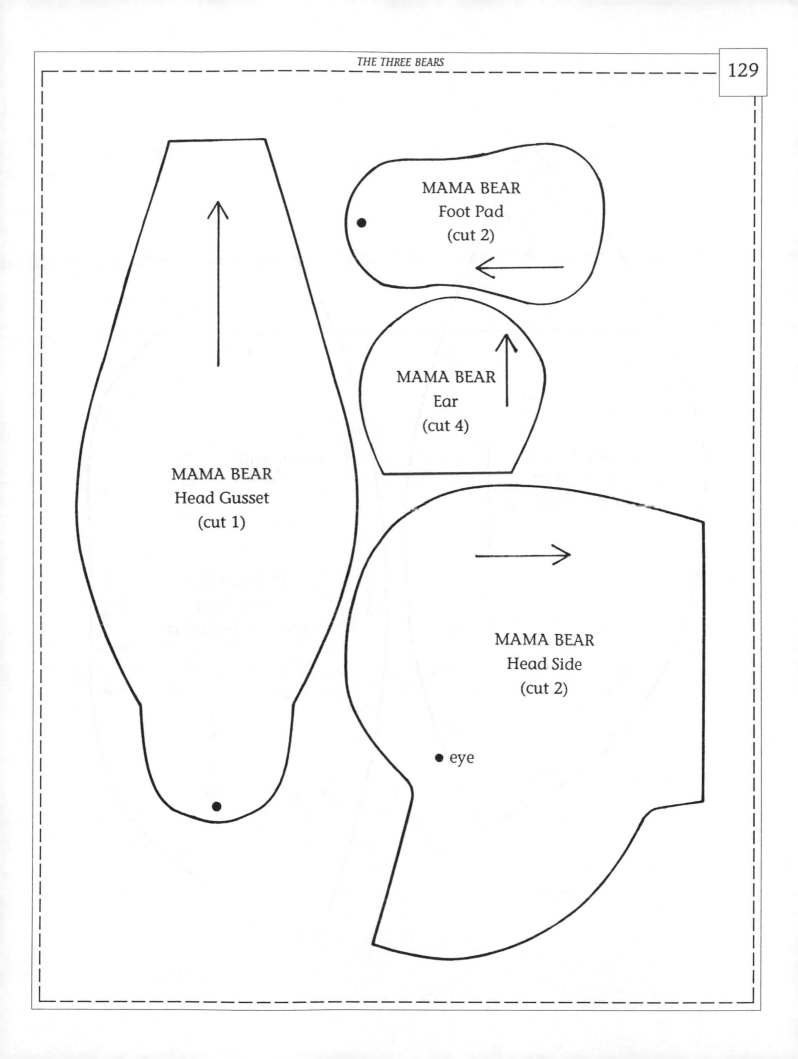

MAMA BEAR
Foot Pad
(cut 2)

MAMA BEAR
Ear
(cut 4)

MAMA BEAR
Head Gusset
(cut 1)

MAMA BEAR
Head Side
(cut 2)

● eye

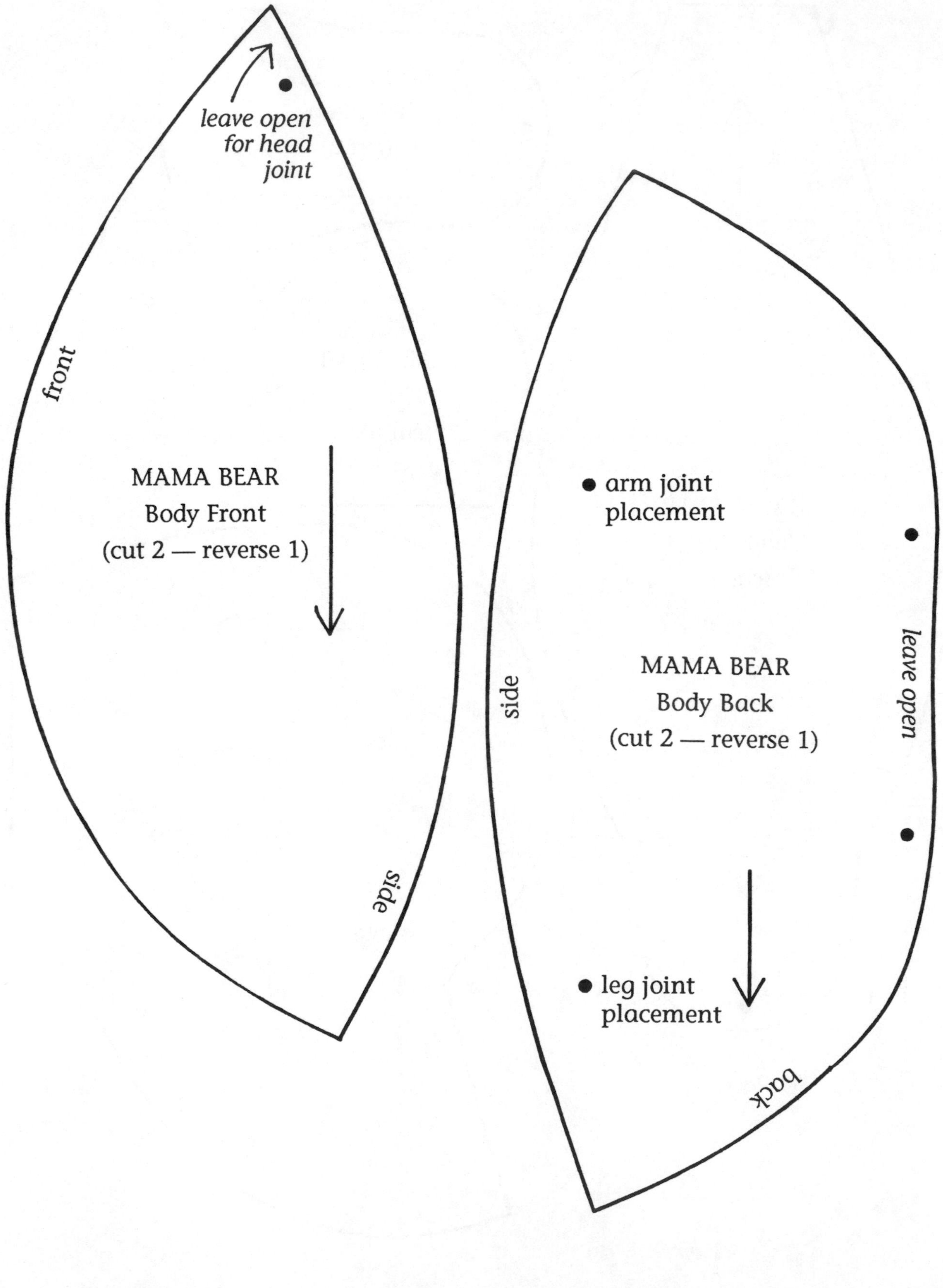

leave open
for head
joint

front

MAMA BEAR
Body Front
(cut 2 — reverse 1)

side

● arm joint
placement

side

leave open

MAMA BEAR
Body Back
(cut 2 — reverse 1)

● leg joint
placement

back

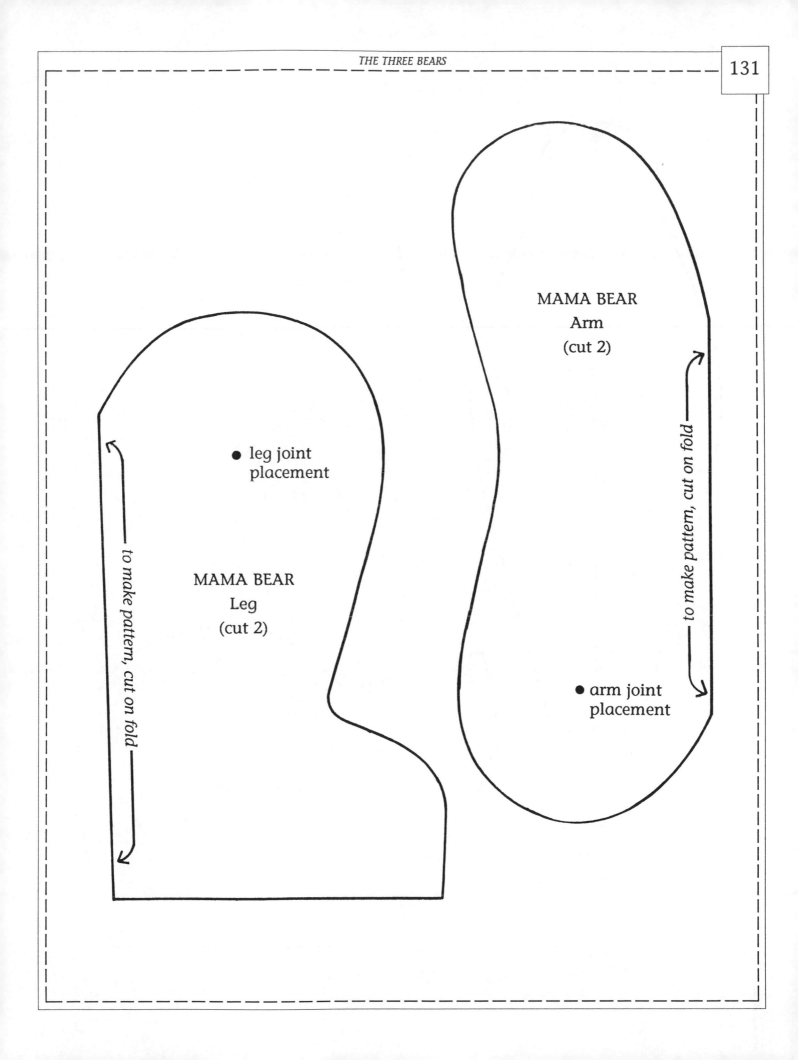

MAMA BEAR
Arm
(cut 2)

to make pattern, cut on fold

● arm joint
placement

● leg joint
placement

MAMA BEAR
Leg
(cut 2)

to make pattern, cut on fold

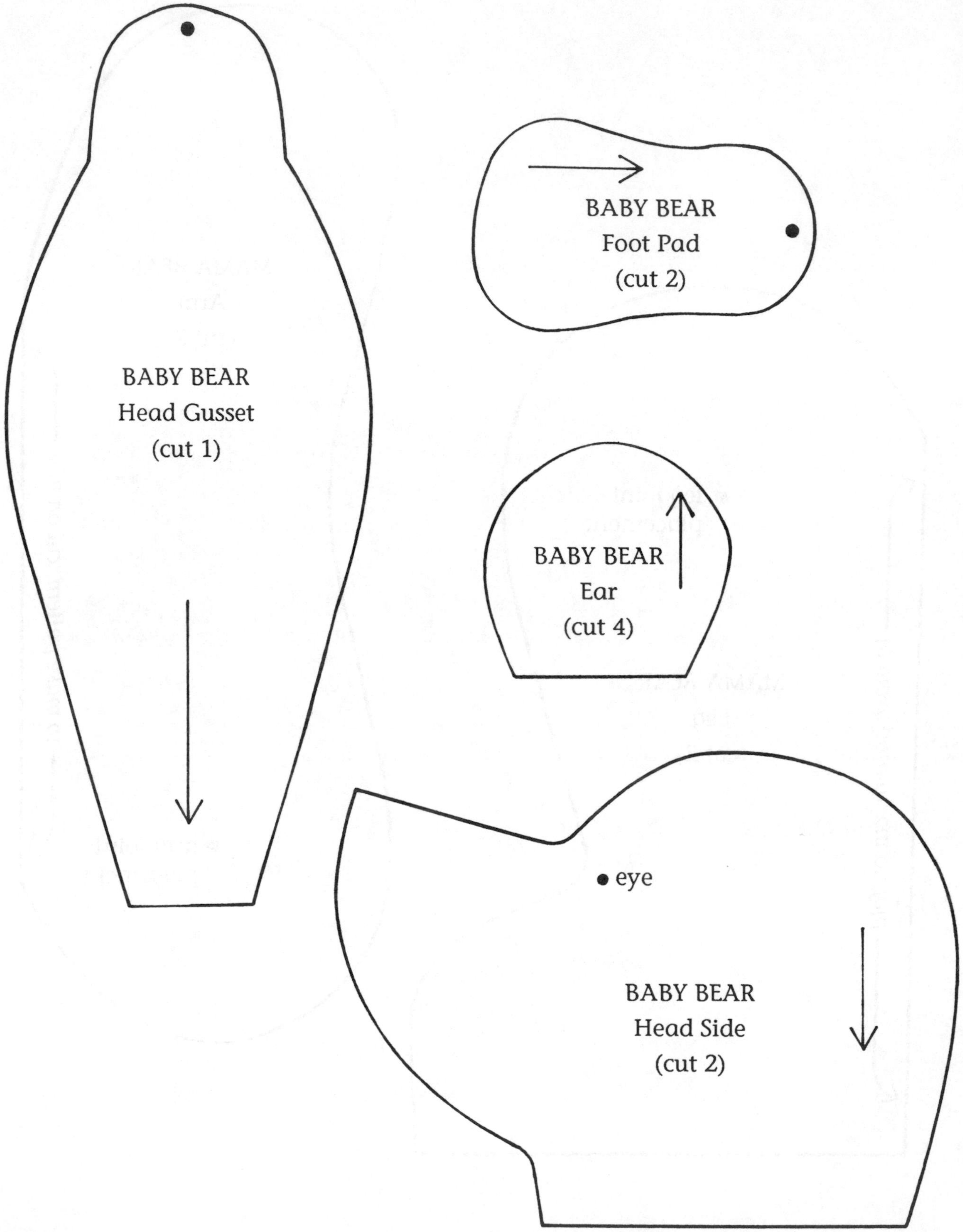

BABY BEAR
Head Gusset
(cut 1)

BABY BEAR
Foot Pad
(cut 2)

BABY BEAR
Ear
(cut 4)

• eye

BABY BEAR
Head Side
(cut 2)

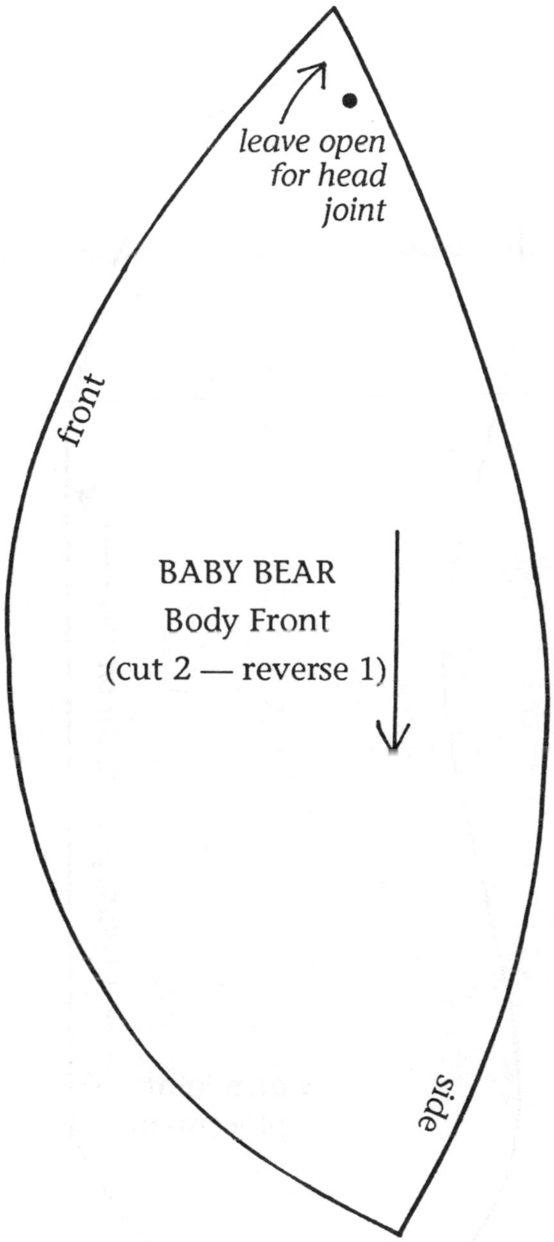

*leave open
for head
joint*

front

BABY BEAR
Body Front
(cut 2 — reverse 1)

side

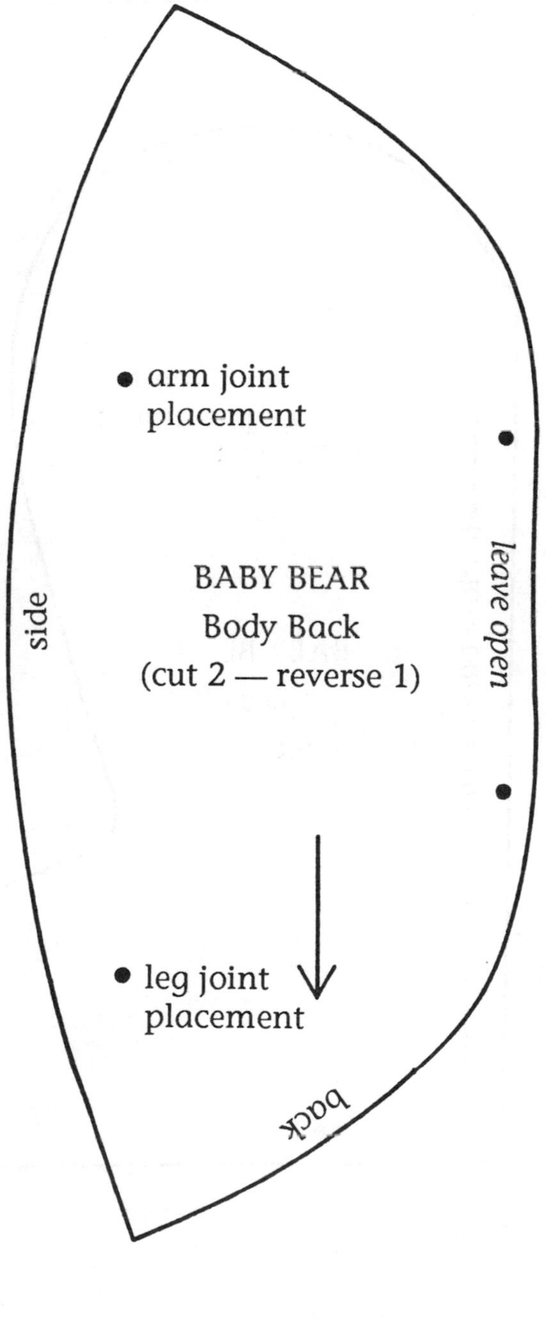

• arm joint
placement

side

BABY BEAR
Body Back
(cut 2 — reverse 1)

leave open

• leg joint
placement

back

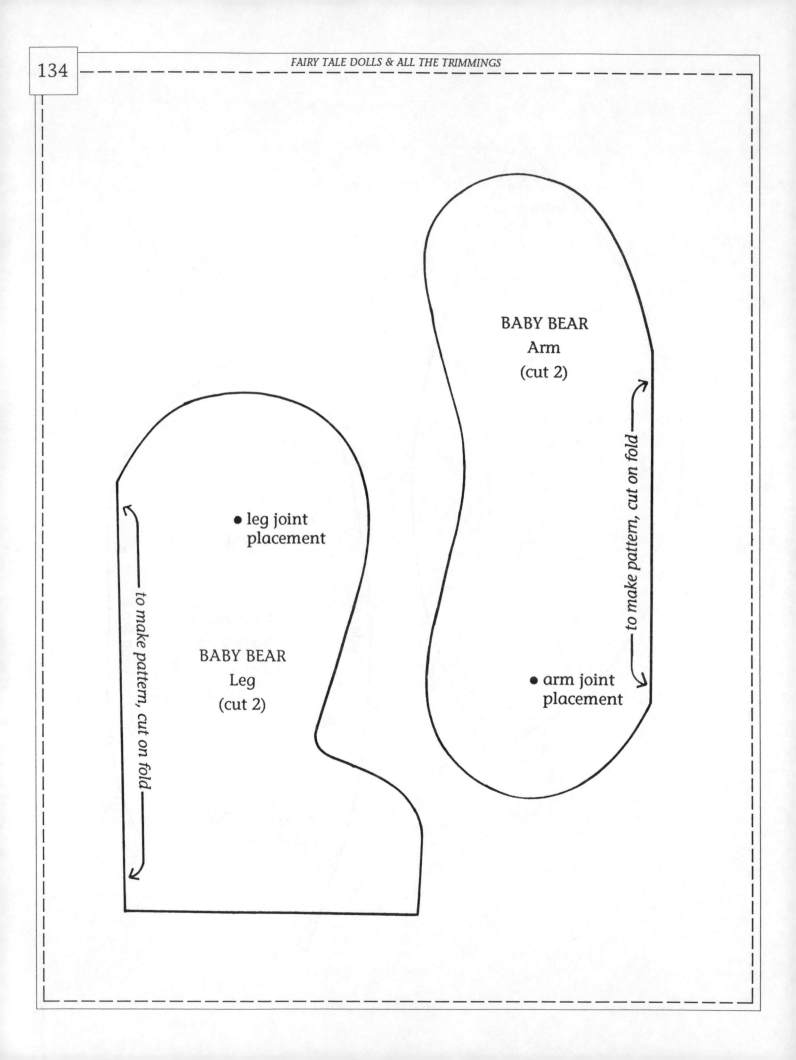

BABY BEAR
Arm
(cut 2)

to make pattern, cut on fold

● arm joint
placement

● leg joint
placement

BABY BEAR
Leg
(cut 2)

to make pattern, cut on fold

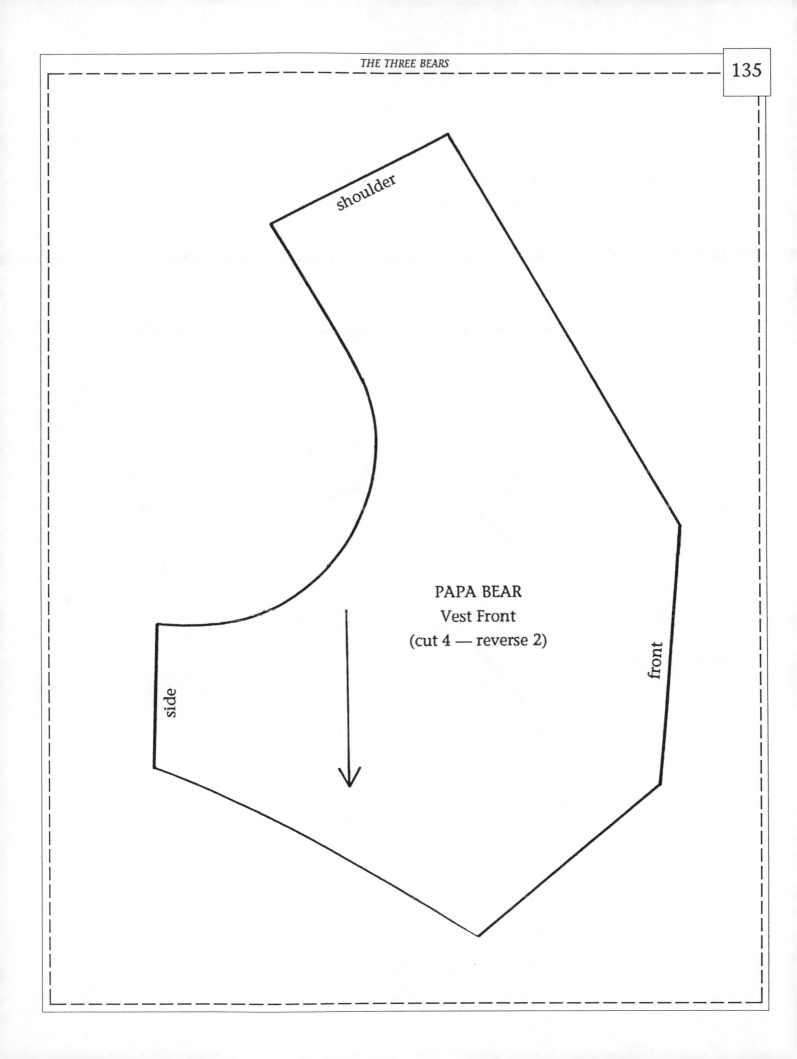

shoulder

side

front

PAPA BEAR
Vest Front
(cut 4 — reverse 2)

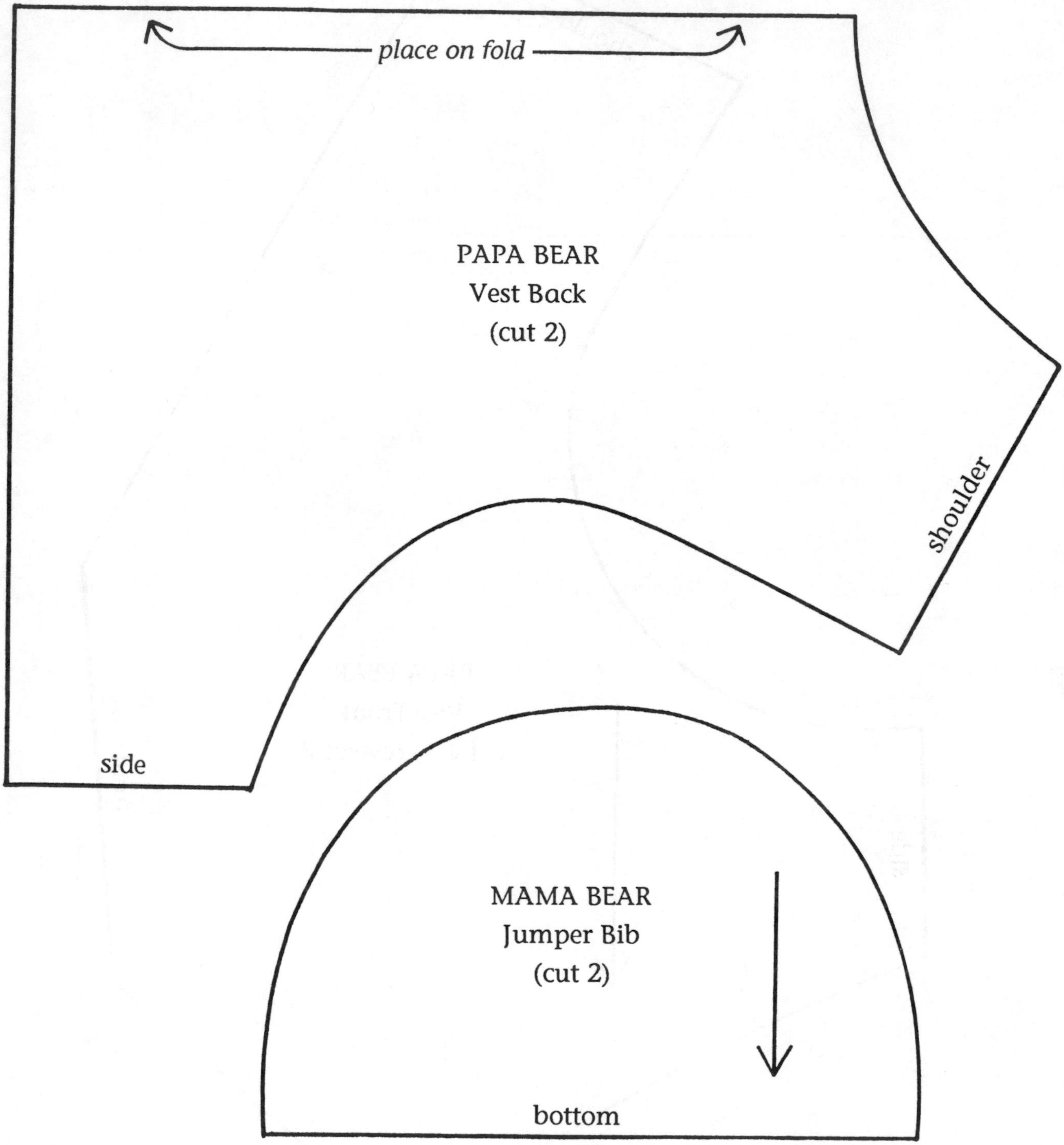

place on fold

PAPA BEAR
Vest Back
(cut 2)

shoulder

side

MAMA BEAR
Jumper Bib
(cut 2)

bottom

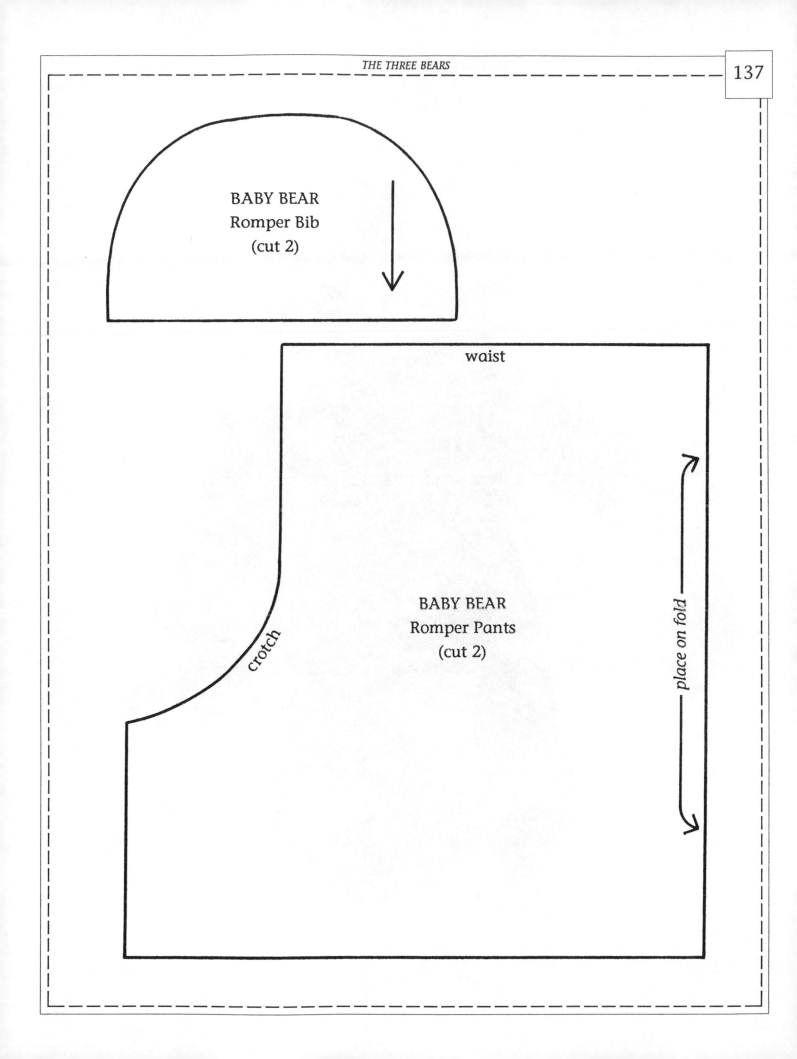

BABY BEAR
Romper Bib
(cut 2)

waist

crotch

BABY BEAR
Romper Pants
(cut 2)

place on fold

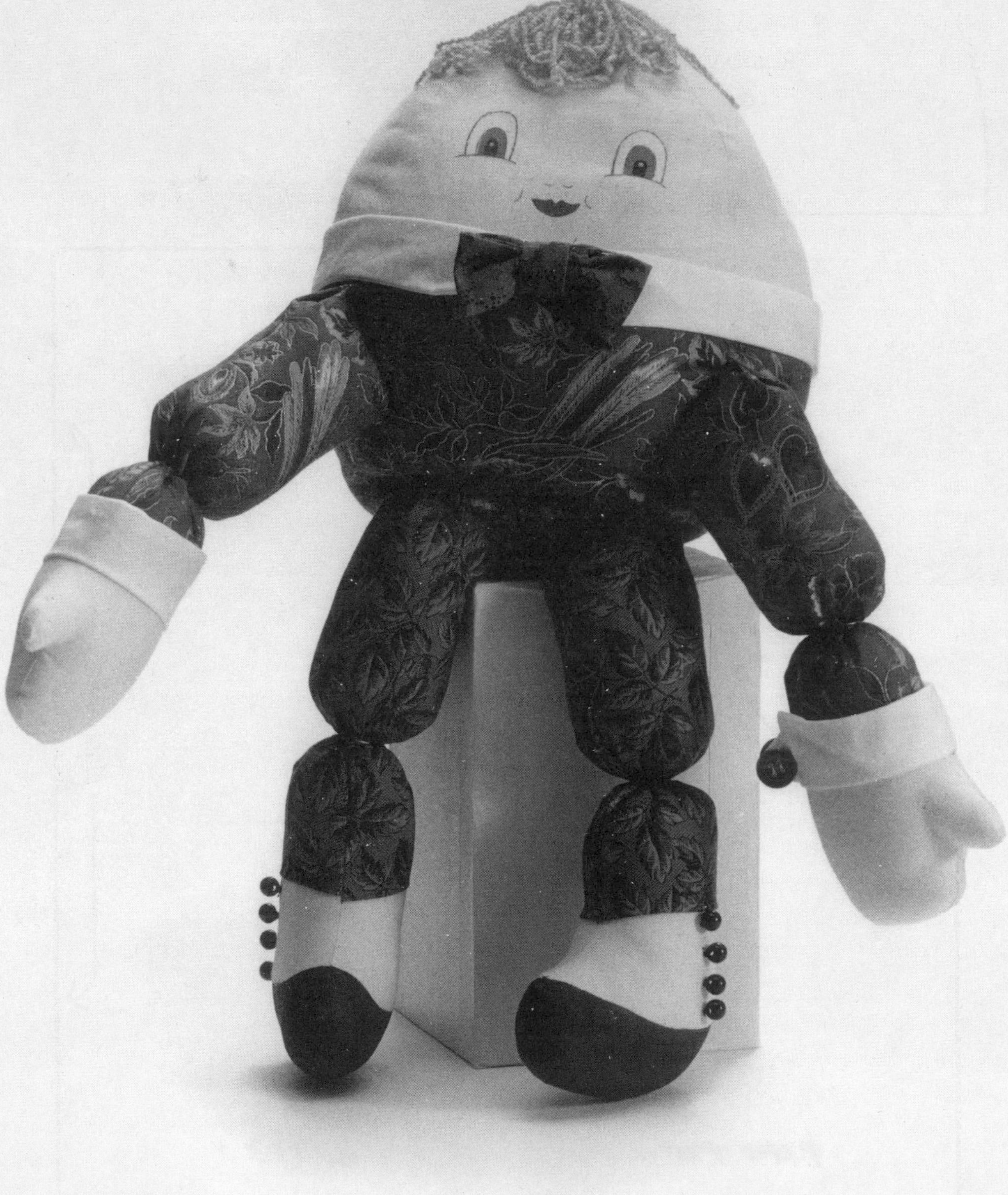

♥

Humpty Dumpty

Jolly old Humpty Dumpty appears oblivious to the fate awaiting him. But perhaps this egghead is smarter than we think. This Humpty is constructed from unfracturable fabric, and he is easy to make. His clothing is stitched as part of his body and his spats are painted on. He measures $18\frac{1}{2}$" tall when standing and sits $10\frac{1}{2}$" high.

♥

MATERIALS

¹/₂ yard muslin for body	Polyester fiberfill stuffing
Matching thread	Acrylic craft paint: black, red, blue (or brown or green, for eyes), and white
¹/₄ yard clothing fabric for body and sleeves	Brown or black fabric marker (see the Basics and Sources)
¹/₄ yard coordinating fabric for pants	Eight ¹/₄" round, black shank buttons
¹/₄ yard white cotton fabric for legs, collar, and cuffs	Four ³/₈" gold shank buttons
Scraps of fabric for bow tie	Scraps of yarn for hair

INSTRUCTIONS

Note: All seam allowances are ¹/₄" unless directed otherwise. Seam allowances are included in patterns.

Prepare the patterns and cut and mark the fabric as instructed in the Basics. From the body clothing fabric, cut two 6¹/₂" x 7¹/₄" rectangles for the sleeves and cut two 6¹/₂" x 7¹/₄" rectangles from the pants legs fabric. Cut two rectangles for the bow tie, one 3" x 6 ¹/₂" and one 1³/₄" x 2¹/₂".

1. As instructed in the Basics, trace the face onto one muslin body piece.

2. Place the suit, sleeve, and pant leg fabric pieces over the body, arm, and leg pieces along the marked lines as shown, right sides facing the muslin.

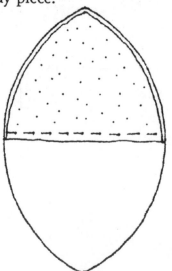

Using a ¹/₄" seam allowance, stitch the clothing fabrics to the body, leg, and arm pieces as shown.

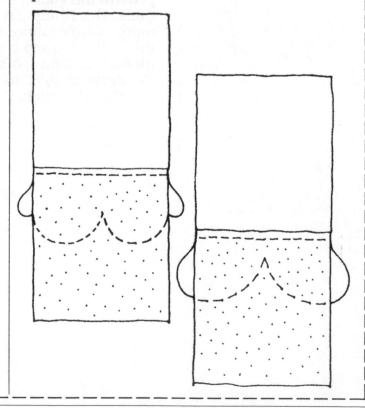

Fold the clothing fabric so its wrong side meets the muslin and the raw edges match those of the muslin body piece. Press in place.

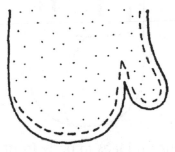

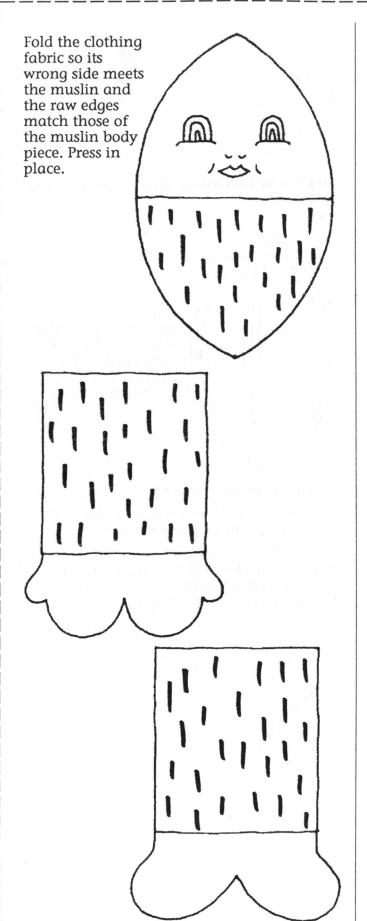

3. Right sides together, fold an arm in half. Stitch, leaving the top open. To make a smooth seam, use small stitches around thumb.

Trim seam allowances to $1/8$". Clip into the V at the thumb. Secure with a drop of Fray Check™. Repeat for the other arm.

Turn arms right side out. Stuff arms to about $4^1/2$" from the tips of the fingers. Tie a heavy thread around the arm as shown. Continue stuffing to about 1" from the top, open raw edges. Baste the openings at the tops of the arms closed.

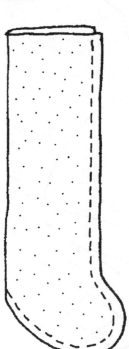

4. Right sides together, fold a leg piece in half. Stitch, leaving the top open. Trim seam allowances to $1/8$". Repeat for the second leg.

Turn legs right sides out. Stuff to about 1" from the top, open edges of the legs. Fold the tops of the legs as shown. Baste.

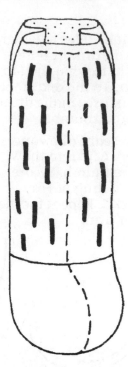

5. Pin and baste arms and legs to body front (the body piece with the face drawn on it) as shown.

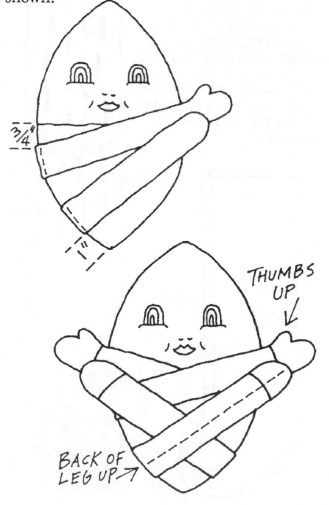

3/4"

THUMBS UP ↙

BACK OF LEG UP →

Right sides facing, pin and stitch two body pieces together. Repeat for the other two body pieces. Don't worry about matching the clothing fabric edges precisely; they will be covered by the collar anyway.

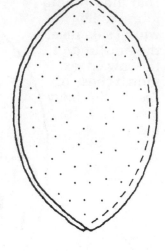

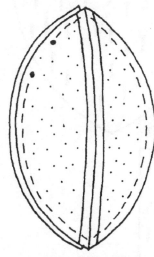

Pin the two sets of body pieces together. Stitch, leaving a 4"-long opening for turning and stuffing as shown.

Trim seam allowances to 1/8".

6. Turn body right side out. Stuff the body. Ladder stitch the opening in the body closed.

7. Fold the collar and cuffs along the fold-line, right sides together. Stitch as shown, leaving openings for turning.

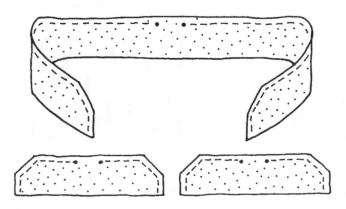

Turn right sides out. Press. Slip stitch openings closed.

Stitch collar to Humpty's body as shown. Fold down.

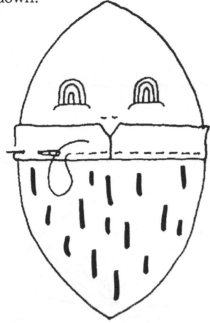

Stitch cuffs to ends of sleeves as shown. Fold back to sleeve.

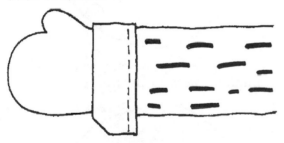

Stitch gold buttons to cuffs.

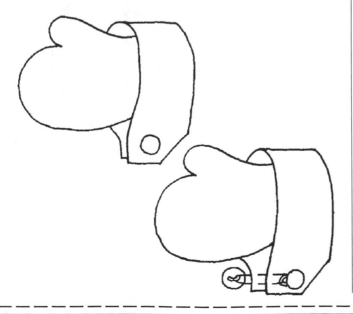

8. Fold the larger tie rectangle in half lengthwise, right sides facing. Stitch three sides of tie as shown, leaving an opening in the stitching for turning. Turn right side out. Press.

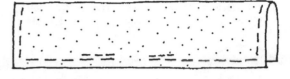

Fold smaller tie rectangle in half lengthwise. Stitch the long edges together. Turn right side out.

Fold tie as shown.

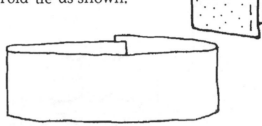

Put the tie together as shown. Secure by stitching it together at the back.

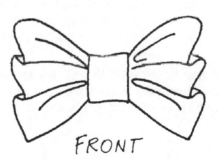

FRONT

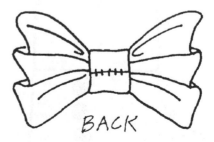

BACK

Stitch tie to Humpty.

9. Paint the whites of Humpty's eyes first. Let them dry while you paint his lips red. When the white paint is dry, paint the eyes blue (or other color). When the blue is dry, add the black pupil. When this is dry, add a tiny white dot to the pupil as a highlight.

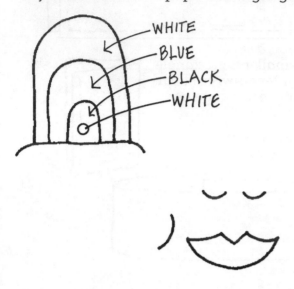

Paint the lips red.

Redraw Humpty's face with the permanent pen over the pencil markings. Fill in the eyebrows, outline the eyes, and go over the nose.

10. Paint the bottom of Humpty's shoes black. Sew the black buttons at the marked dots on the sides of Humpty's shoes.

11. Loop yarn about eight times to make a 6"-long loop as shown.

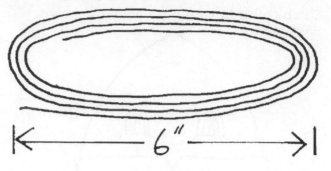

Stitch the center of the yarn loop to the top of Humpty's head.

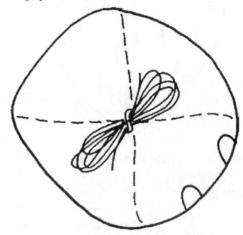

Repeat three times, sewing the groups of hair at different axes as shown.

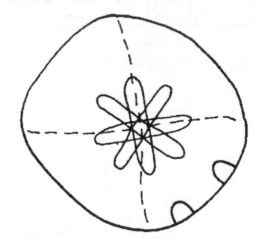

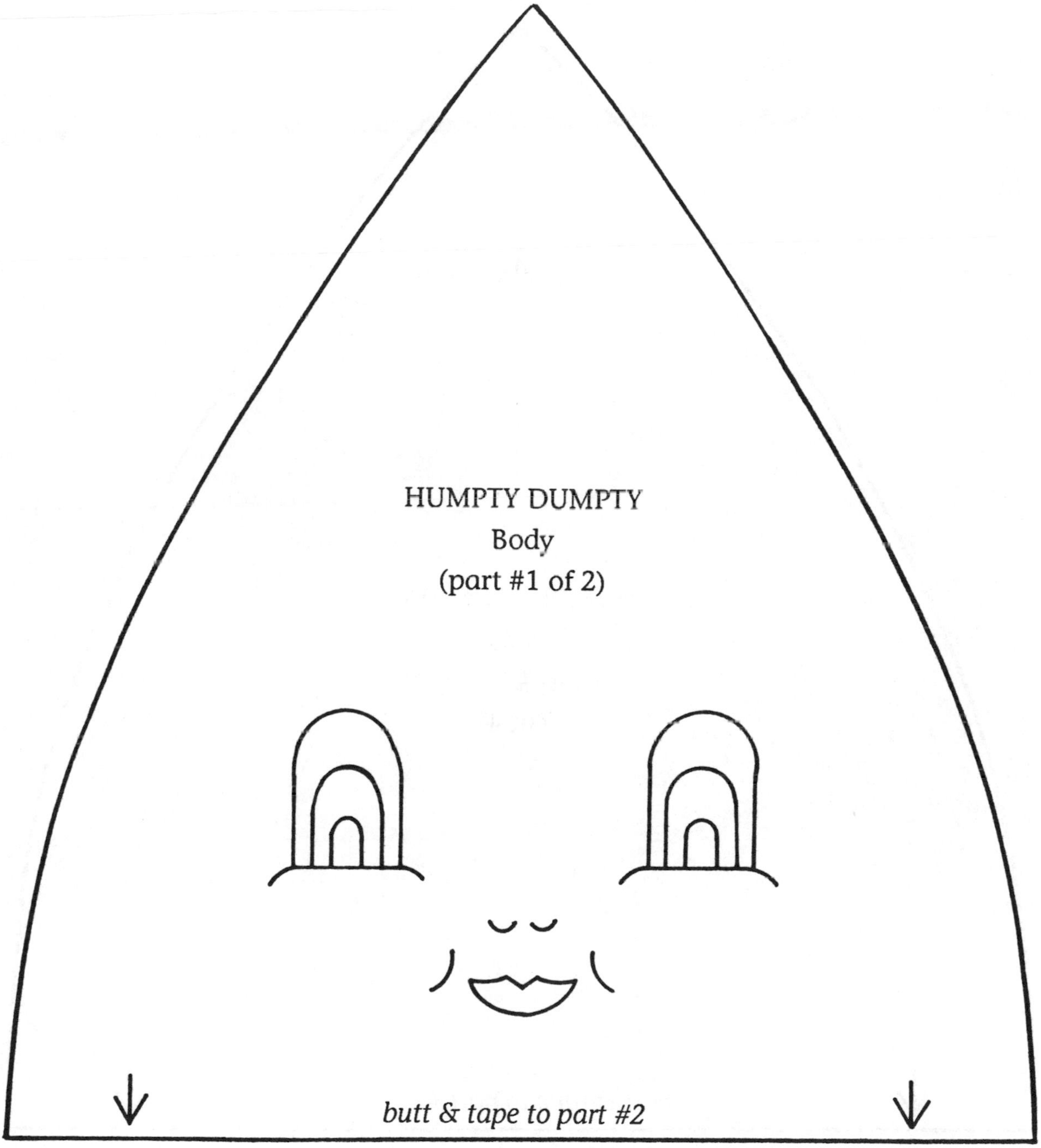

HUMPTY DUMPTY
Body
(part #1 of 2)

↓ *butt & tape to part #2* ↓

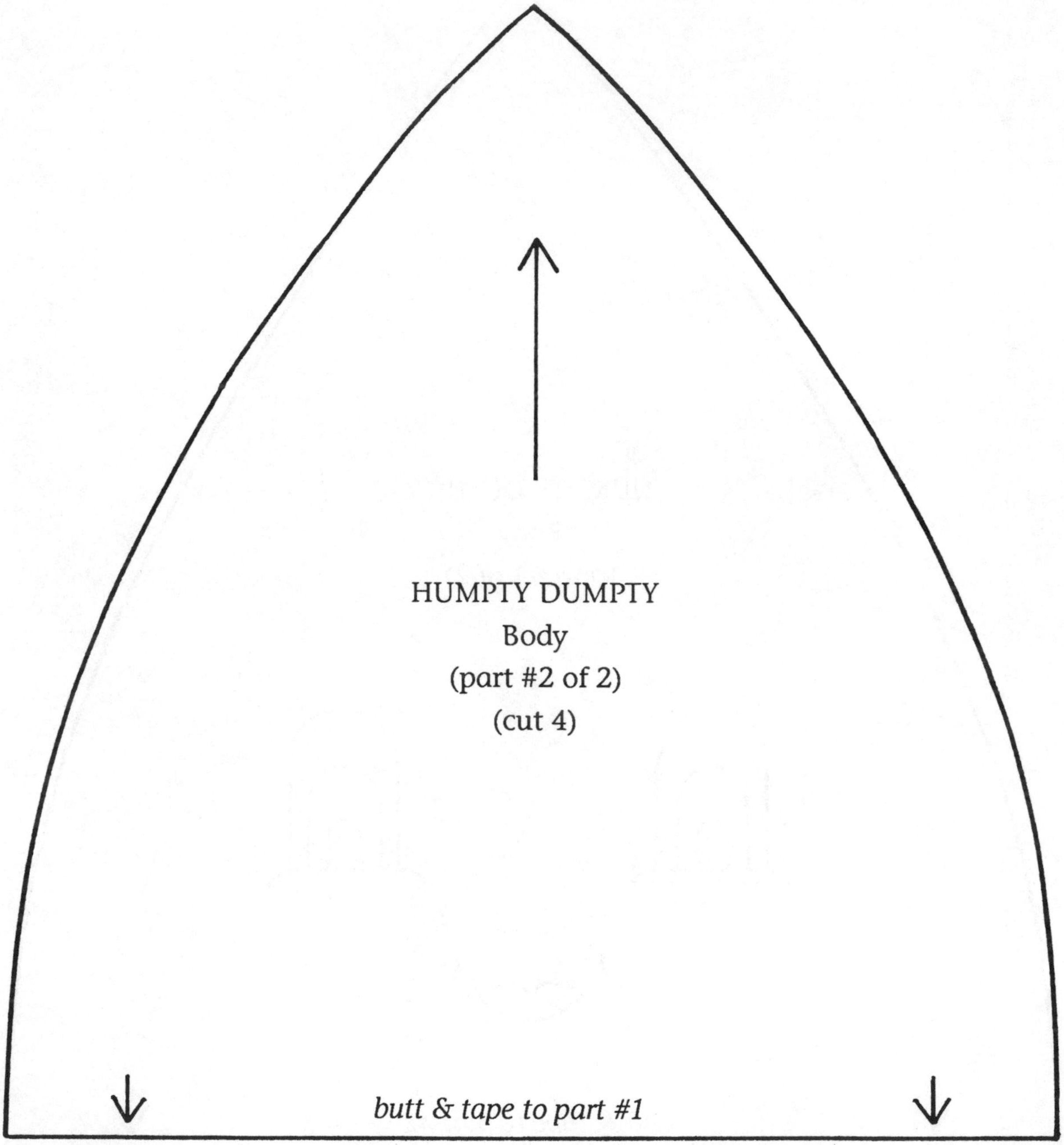

HUMPTY DUMPTY
Body
(part #2 of 2)
(cut 4)

↑

↓   *butt & tape to part #1*   ↓

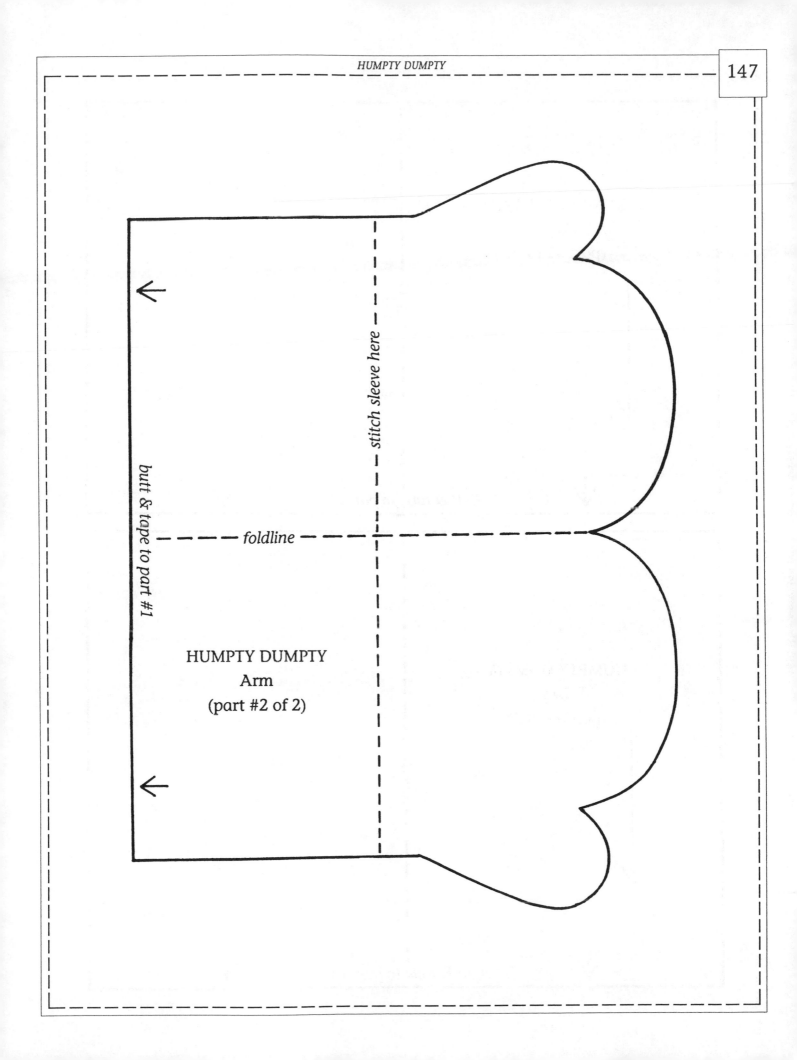

stitch sleeve here

butt & tape to part #1

foldline

HUMPTY DUMPTY
Arm
(part #2 of 2)

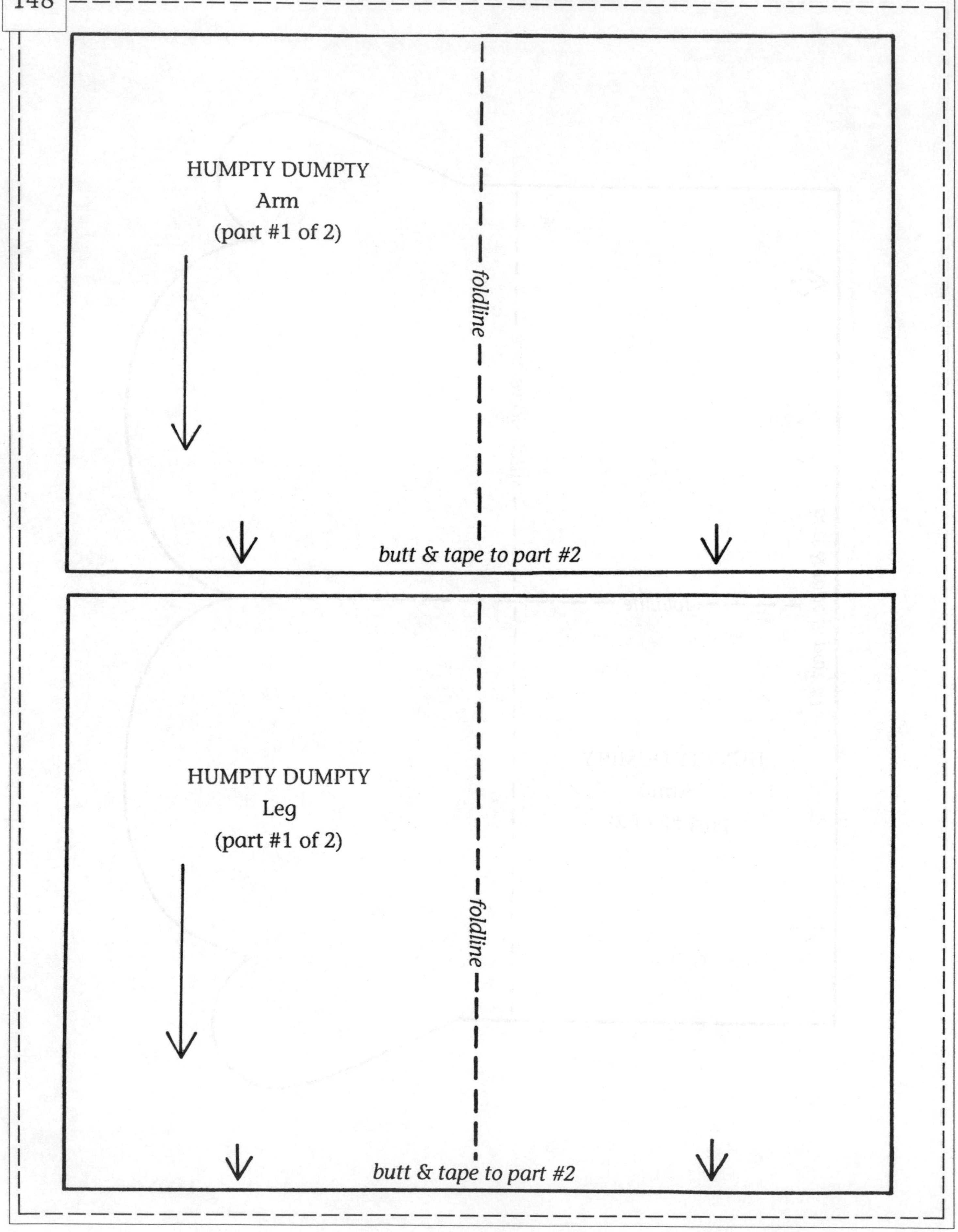

HUMPTY DUMPTY
Arm
(part #1 of 2)

foldline

butt & tape to part #2

HUMPTY DUMPTY
Leg
(part #1 of 2)

foldline

butt & tape to part #2

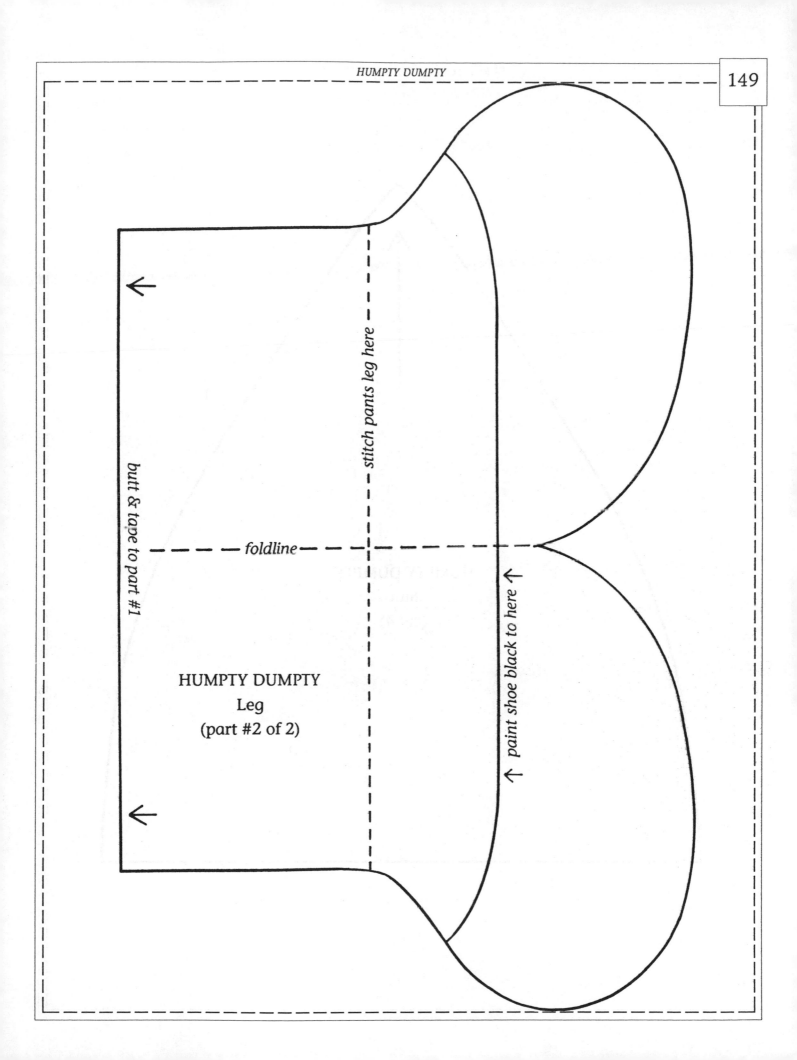

butt & tape to part #1

foldline

stitch pants leg here

↑ paint shoe black to here ↑

HUMPTY DUMPTY
Leg
(part #2 of 2)

HUMPTY DUMPTY
Suit
(cut 4)

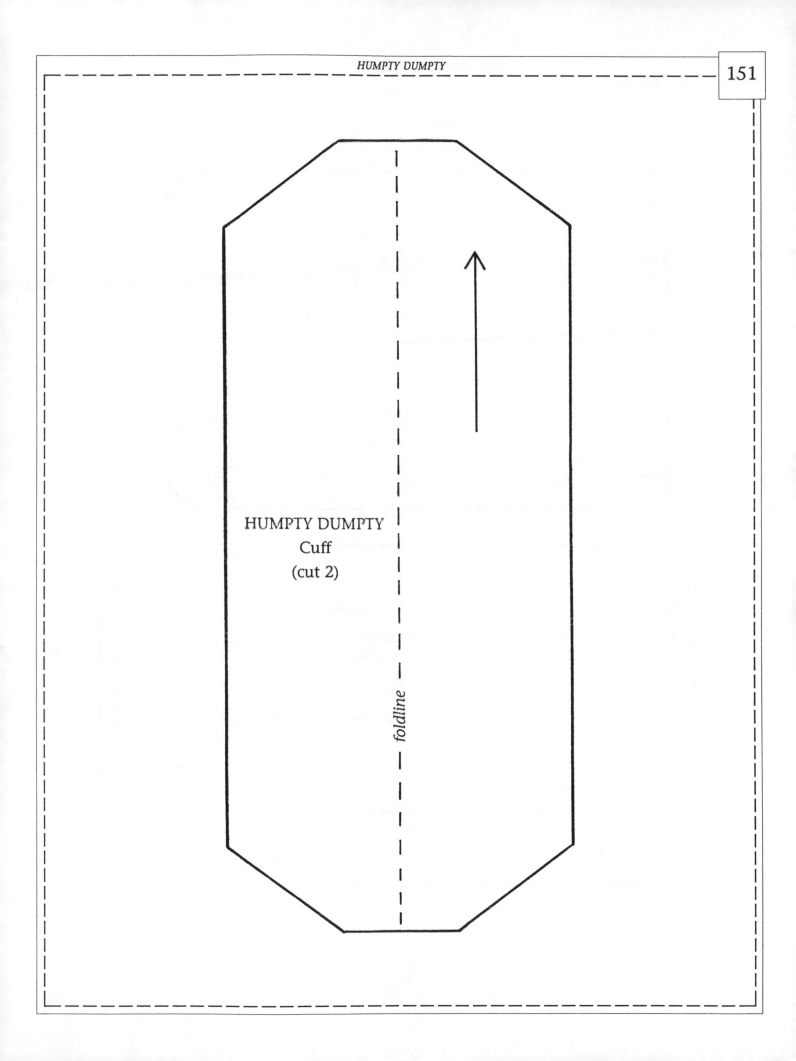

HUMPTY DUMPTY
Cuff
(cut 2)

foldline

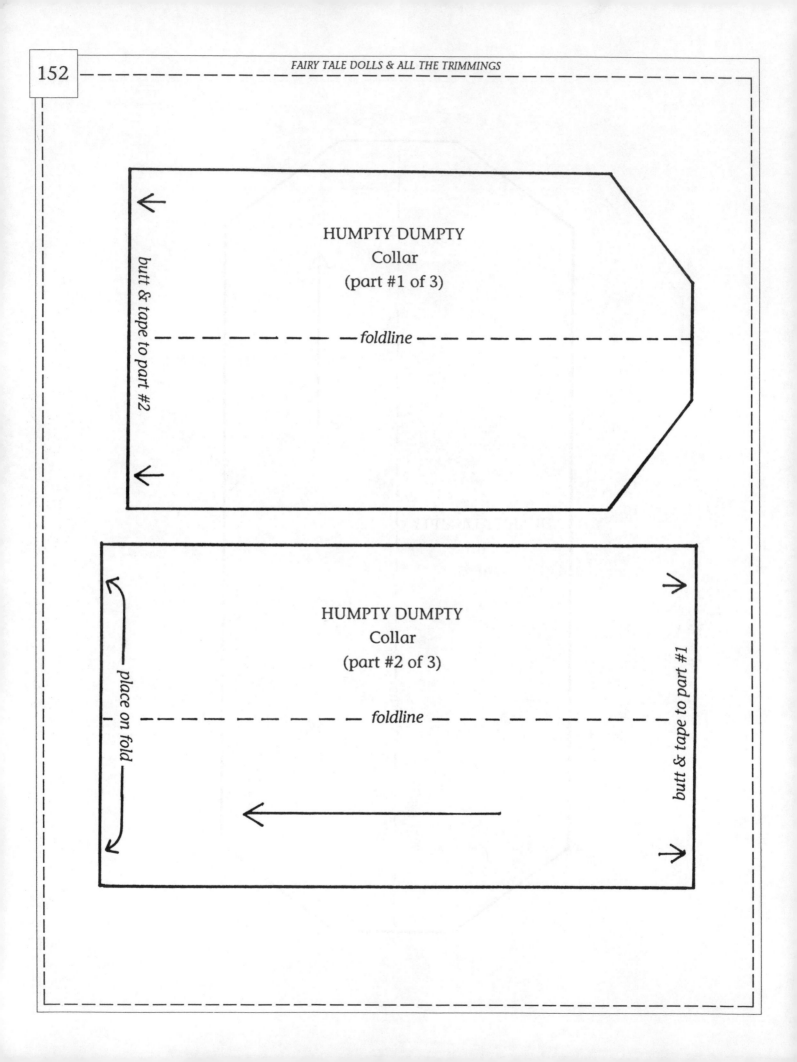

HUMPTY DUMPTY
Collar
(part #1 of 3)

butt & tape to part #2

— foldline —

HUMPTY DUMPTY
Collar
(part #2 of 3)

place on fold

butt & tape to part #1

— foldline —

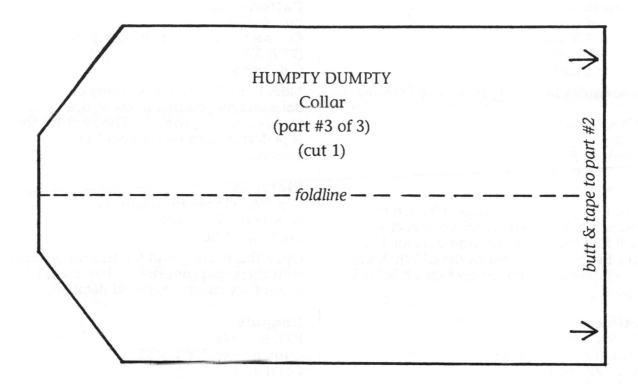

HUMPTY DUMPTY
Collar
(part #3 of 3)
(cut 1)

— *foldline* —

butt & tape to part #2

Collar Pattern Assembly:

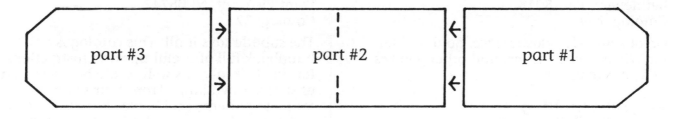

part #3 → part #2 ← part #1

 Sources

by Diane
1126 Ivon Ave.
Endicott, NY 13760
(607) 754-0391
Catalog: $1.50

Diane carries fur and eyes for The Three Bears.

CR'S Crafts
Box 8
Leland, IA 50453
(515) 567-3652
Catalog: $2

This catalog is full of a large selection of goodies for dollmaking and general crafts. You'll find the fur, joints, and eyes for The Three Bears here as well as the 6" Witch's hat and 5½" woven white bonnet for Little Bo Peep.

Clotilde, Inc.
P.O. Box 22312
Ft. Lauderdale, FL 33332
1-800-772-2891
Catalog: $1

Here you will find every sewing notion imaginable, all discounted at least twenty percent. And a great price on the Pigma™ 01 pen in black and brown.

Home Sew
Bethlehem, PA 18018
Catalog: Free

Great source for elastic, lace, gold buckles for Witch's shoes, trims, and other goodies at fantastic prices.

Keepsake Quilting
Route 25, P.O. Box 1618
Centre Harbor, NH 03226-1618
(603) 253-8731

Shop at home with Keepsake's cotton fabric swatch sets. Choose from the many doll patterns sprinkled throughout the catalog.

National Artcraft Co.
23456 Mercantile Rd.
Beachwood, OH 44122
Catalog: $3

Your dolls will appreciate a little help standing up from this company's doll stands.

Patterncrafts
Box 25370
Colorado Springs, CO 80936-5370
(719) 574-2007
Catalog: $2

More than 700 patterns, many of them for dolls and all pictured in color, are featured in this inspiring catalog. The Stuff-It™ tool is perfect for getting into tight places like fingers.

Platypus
Box 396, Planetarium Station
New York, NY 10024
Catalog: $1.50

Open this catalog and fall in love instantly with these gorgeous dolls. They are all beautifully constructed and detailed.

Ragpats
P.O. Box 175
Caroga Lake, NY 12032
Catalog: $3

Over 200 patterns from the 1930s to 1970s are included in this catalog. All are reprinted directly from the original.

Mimi's Books & Supplies
For the Serious Dollmaker
P.O. Box 662
Point Pleasant, NJ 08742
Catalog: $2

The subtitle says it all. This catalog is a handbook full of useful tips and instructions for the dollmaker as well as the best selection of supplies available. From hair to body fabric to patterns and books, Mimi's catalog is a must. Mimi also publishes a wonderful quarterly magazine. Full of artist profiles, and all the latest tips, tools, and techniques, Let's Talk About Dollmaking offers you an inside seat on all the goings on of the movers and shakers in the cloth doll world.

Bibliography

Cherished Dolls You Can Make For Fun by Better Homes & Gardens Editors, Better Homes & Gardens books.

Cloth Doll Magazine
P.O. Box 1089
Mount Shasta, CA 96067
Subscription: $13.95

Discovering a copy of this magazine in your mailbox is like a visit from a family room full of dollmaking friends. Patterns are included in every issue as well as lots of dollmaking tips and information.

The Cloth Dollmaker's Sourcebook by Diane Patterson Dee, Betterway Publications, Inc., White Hall, VA.

This is a topnotch book for doll and stuffed animal making. Contemporary designers are featured as well as suppliers of materials and accessories.

Cloth Dolls, How to Make Them by Miriam Gourley, The Quilt Digest Press, Gualala, CA, 1989.

Doll Maker's Journal
2900 W. Anderson Lane
#20150, Austin, TX 78757
Quarterly: $15 per year

Reader's Digest Complete Guide to Sewing, Reader's Digest Books.

More good books from
WILLIAMSON PUBLISHING

To order additional copies of **Easy-To-Make Fairy Tale Dolls & All The Trimmings**, please enclose $13.95 per copy plus $2.50 for shipping and handling. Follow "To Order" instructions on the last page. Thank you.

Easy-To-Make CLOTH DOLLS & ALL THE TRIMMINGS
by Jodie Davis

Jodie Davis turns her many talents to making the most adorable and personable cloth dolls imaginable. With her expert directions and clear full-sized patterns, anyone can create these instant friends for a special child or friend. Includes seven 18-inch dolls like Santa, Raggedy Ann, and a clown; a 20-inch baby doll plus complete wardrobe; a 25-inch boy and girl doll plus a wardrobe including sailor suits; and 10 dolls from around the world including a Japanese kimono doll and Amish dolls. Absolutely beautiful and you can do it!

224 pages, 8½ x 11, illustrations and patterns
Quality paperback, $13.95

Easy-to-Make ENDANGERED SPECIES TO STITCH & STUFF
by Jodie Davis

Another wonderful book by the amazing Jodie Davis. Along with making the most adorable stuffed animals such as a loggerhead turtle, spotted owl and bald eagle, you can have wonderful windsocks adorned with these fabulous animals that we all treasure so much. Picture some playful pandas on a black and white windsock or a gorgeous scarlet macaw. And, too, there are instructions for appliqued pillows and beautiful wall-hanging flags of these marvelous creatures. Let Jodie show you how with her step-by-step instructions and full-sized patterns.
192 pages, 8½ x 11, illustrations and patterns
Quality paperback, $13.95

Easy-to-Make TEDDY BEARS & ALL THE TRIMMINGS
by Jodie Davis

Now you can make the most lovable, huggable, plain or fancy teddy bears imaginable, for a fraction of store-bought costs. Step-by-step instructions and easy patterns drawn to actual size for large, soft-bodied bears, quilted bears, and even jointed bears. Plus patterns for clothes, accessories — even teddy bear furniture!

208 pages, 8½ x 11, illustrations and patterns
Quality paperback, $13.95

Easy-To-Make STUFFED ANIMALS & ALL THE TRIMMINGS
by Jodie Davis

With Jodie Davis's complete and easy instructions, creating adorable stuffed animals has never been easier. Whether you are making gifts for children or additions for a special doll collection, these fuzzy animals are sure to delight anyone. Includes 14-inch unicorn, Rudolph doll, and a large assortment of farm animals — complete with clothing patterns!

208 pages, 8½ x 11, illustrations and patterns
Quality paperback, $13.95

THE KIDS' NATURE BOOK
365 Indoor/Outdoor Activities and Experiences
by Susan Milord

Winner of the Parents' Choice Gold Award for learning and doing books, *The Kids' Nature Book* is loved by children, grandparents, and friends alike. Simple projects and activities emphasize fun while quietly reinforcing the wonder of the world we all share. Packed with facts and fun!

160 pages, 11 x 8½, 425 illustrations
Quality paperback, $12.95

EcoArt!
Earth-Friendly Art & Craft Experiences for 3-to 9-year-olds
by Laurie Carlson

What better way to learn to love and care for the Earth than through creative art play! Laurie Carlson's latest book is packed with 150 projects using only recyclable, reusable, or nature's own found art materials. These fabulous activities are sure to please any child!

160 pages, 11 x 8½, 400 illustrations
Quality paperback, $12.95

KIDS CREATE!
Art & Craft Experiences for 3– to 9–year–olds
by Laurie Carlson

What's the most important experience for children ages 3 to 9? Why, to create something by themselves. Carlson provides over 150 creative experiences ranging from making dinosaur sculptures to clay cactus gardens, from butterfly puppets to windsocks. Plenty of help for the parents working with the kids, too! A delightfully innovative book.

160 pages, 11 x 8½, over 400 illustrations
Quality paperback, $12.95

KIDS COOK!
Fabulous Food for the Whole Family
by Sarah Williamson and Zachary Williamson

Kids Cook! is filled with over 150 recipes for great tasting foods that kids ages 8 and up can cook for themselves and for their families and friends, too. Recipes from sections like "It's the Berries!" "Pasta Perfect,""Home Alone," "Side Orders," Babysitter's Bonanza," and "Best Bets for Brunch" include real, healthy foods — not cutesy recipes that are no fun to eat. Plus Nutri Notes, Safety First, and plenty of special menus for Father's Day, Grandma's Teatime, picnics, and parties. One terrific book!

160 pages, 11 x 8^1/$_2$, over 150 recipes, illustrations
Quality paperback, $12.95

KIDS & WEEKENDS!
Creative Ways to Make Special Days
by Avery Hart and Paul Mantell

Packed with truly creative ways to play, have fun, learn, grow, and build self-esteem and positive relationships, this book is a must for every parent, grandparent, baby-sitter, and teacher. Hart and Mantell will inspire us all to transform some part of every weekend — even if it is only 30 minutes — into a special experience. Everything from back-yard nature to putting on a magic show to creating a bird sanctuary to writing a book about yourself to environmentally sound activities indoors and out. Whatever your interests, no matter how busy you are, kids and their families will savor special weekend moments.

176 pages, 11 x 8^1/$_2$, over 400 illustrations
Quality paperback, $12.95

ADVENTURES IN ART
Art & Craft Experiences for 7- to 14-year-olds
by Susan Milord

Imagine an art book that encourages children to explore, to experience, to touch and to see, to learn and to create . . . imagine a true adventure in art. Here's a book that teaches artisans' skills without stifling creativity. Covers making handmade papers, puppets, masks, paper seascapes, seed art, tin can lantern, berry ink, still life, silk screen, batiking, carving, and so much more. Perfect for the older child. Let the adventure begin!

160 pages, 11 x 8^1/$_2$, 500 illustrations
Quality paperback, $12.95

KIDS LEARN AMERICA!
Bringing Geography to Life with People, Places, & History
by Patricia Gordon and Reed C. Snow

Designed to help increase "geo-literacy," Kids Learn America! is not about memorizing. This creative and exciting new book is about making every region of our country come alive from within, about being connected to the earth and the people across this great expanse called America. •Activities and games targeted to the 50 states plus D.C. and Puerto Rico •The environment and natural resources •Geographic comparisons •Fascinating facts, famous people and places of each region. Let us all join together — kids, parents, friends, teachers, grandparents — and put America, its geography, its history, and its heritage back on the map!

176 pages, 11 x 8½, maps, illustrations
Quality paperback, $12.95

DOING CHILDREN'S MUSEUMS
A Guide to 265 Hands-On Museums, Expanded and Updated
by Joanne Cleaver

Turn an ordinary day into a spontaneous "vacation" by taking a child to some of the 265 participatory children's museums, discovery rooms, and nature centers covered in this highly acclaimed, one-of-a-kind book. Filled with museum specifics to help you pick and plan the perfect place for the perfect day, Cleaver has created a most valuable resource for anyone who loves kids!

272 pages, 6 x 9
Quality paperback, $13.95

PARENTS ARE TEACHERS, TOO
Enriching Your Child's First Six Years
by Claudia Jones

Winner of the Parents' Choice Seal of Approval! Be the best teacher your child ever has. Jones shares hundreds of ways to help any child learn in playful home situations. Lots on developing reading, writing, math skills. Plenty on creative and critical thinking, too. A book you'll love using!

192 pages, 6 x 9, illustrations
Quality paperback, $9.95

MORE PARENTS ARE TEACHERS, TOO
Encouraging Your 6- to 12-Year-Old
by Claudia Jones

Winner of the Parents' Choice Seal of Approval! Help your children be the best they can be! When parents are involved, kids do better. When kids do better, they feel better, too. Here's a wonderfully creative book of ideas, activities, teaching methods and more to help you help your children over the rough spots and share in their growing joy in achieving. Plenty on reading, writing, math, problem-solving, creative thinking. Everything for parents who want to help but not push their children.

224 pages, 6 x 9, illustrations
Quality paperback, $10.95

THE HOMEWORK SOLUTION
by Linda Agler Sonna

Put homework responsibilities where they belong — in the student's lap! Here it is! The simple remedy for the millions of parents who are tired of waging the never-ending nightly battle over kids' homework. Dr. Sonna's "One Step Solution" will relieve parents, kids, and their siblings of the ongoing problem within a single month.

192 pages, 6 x 9
Quality paperback, $10.95

THE BROWN BAG COOKBOOK
Nutritious Portable Lunches for Kids and Grown-Ups
by Sara Sloan

Now in its ninth printing this popular book has more than 1,000 brown bag lunch ideas with 150 recipes for simple, quick, nutritious lunches that kids will love. Breakfast ideas, too! The more people care what they eat, the more popular this book becomes.

192 pages, 8¼ x 7¼, illustrations
Quality paperback, $9.95

GOLDE'S HOMEMADE COOKIES
by Golde Soloway

Over 50,000 copies of this marvelous cookbook have been sold. Now its in its second edition with 135 of the most delicious cookie recipes imaginable. *Publishers Weekly* says, "Cookies are her chosen realm and how sweet a world it is to visit." You're sure to agree!

162 pages, 8¼ x 7¼ , illustrations
Quality paperback, $8.95

To Order:

At your bookstore or order directly from Williamson Publishing. We accept Visa and MasterCard (please include number and expiration date), or send check to:

Williamson Publishing Company
Church Hill Road, P.O. Box 185
Charlotte, Vermont 05445

Toll-free phone orders with credit cards:
1-800-234-8791

Please add $2.50 for postage and handling. Satisfaction is guaranteed or full refund without questions or quibbles.